2O0 pies and tarts

hamlyn | all color cookbook

200 pies and tarts

Sara Lewis

An Hachette UK Company
www.hachette.co.uk

First published in Great Britain in 2012 by Hamlyn
a division of Octopus Publishing Group Ltd
Endeavour House, 189 Shaftesbury Avenue
London WC2H 8JY
www.octopusbooks.co.uk

Distributed in the US by Hachette Book Group USA
237 Park Avenue, New York NY 10017 USA
www.octopusbooksusa.com

Distributed in Canada by Canadian Manda Group
165 Dufferin Street, Toronto, Ontario, Canada M6K 3H6

ISBN 978-0-60062-397-7

A CIP catalogue record for this book is available from the
British Library

Printed and bound in China

10 9 8 7 6 5 4 3 2 1

Standard level spoon and cup measurements are used in all
recipes unless otherwise indicated.

Ovens should be preheated to the specified temperature—
if using a convection oven, follow the manufacturer's
instructions for adjusting the time and temperature.

Fresh herbs should be used unless otherwise stated.
Large eggs should be used unless otherwise stated.

Some recipes are specified for those following a gluten-free
diet. It is prudent to check the labels of all prepared
ingredients for the inclusion of any ingredients that may
contain gluten because different brands may vary.

This book includes dishes made with nuts and nut derivatives.
It is advisable for those with known allergic reactions to nuts
and nut derivatives or those who may be potentially vulnerable
to these allergies, such as pregnant and nursing mothers,
people with certain chronic conditions, the elderly, babies,
and children, to avoid dishes made with these. It is prudent to
check the labels of all prepared ingredients for the possible
inclusion of nut derivatives.

contents

introduction

Home baking is making a resurgence. With so many people living busy lives, rediscovering the joys of cooking can be both relaxing and rewarding—and home-cooked dishes often taste much better than the store-bought versions. Over the next few pages you will find a range of recipes from tiny bite-size pies and tarts made in a mini muffin pan to picnic pies that can be added to school or work lunch bags, savory tarts for a midweek dinner or a special Saturday supper, to melt-in-the-mouth fruit pies and tarts that will remind you of vacations abroad or perhaps nostalgic memories of mom's or

granny's cooking. There is also a chapter for gluten-free pies and tarts, so that those on a special diet won't feel left out. Making pastry is not as difficult as some new cooks may think; the secret is to have a good set of standard kitchen measuring spoons and cups so that you can measure the ingredients accurately. You also need to chill the dough after making it and to roll out on a surface lightly dusted with flour so that the dough doesn't stick. However, if you don't have time to make your own pastry, don't worry; you can still make the recipes—just cheat a little and use ready-to-bake pastries from the stores.

Basic flaky pastry dough

A great versatile, everyday dough. The secret is to keep everything cool, to use a light touch, and to handle as little as possible. Add just enough water to mix, allowing 1 teaspoon for about every 3 tablespoons of flour—too much and the pastry will be sticky and taste hard when baked.

Makes 15 oz

Enough to make:

- A deep 8 inch pie with a lattice decoration
- Or six 14 inch tarts
- Or 12 muffin-size tarts
- Or line four 5 inch tart pans
- Or line a 9½ inch × 1 inch deep tart pan

2 cups **all-purpose flour**
4 tablespoons **butter** plus ¼ cup **shortening** or **lard**, or ¼ lb (1 stick) **butter**, diced
2½–3 tablespoons **cold water**
salt

Add the flour and a pinch of salt to a large mixing bowl. Add the fats and rub them into the flour with your fingertips or use a freestanding electric mixer until the mixture resembles fine crumbs.

Gradually mix in just enough water to enable the crumbs to be squeezed together to form a soft but not sticky dough.

Knead very lightly until smooth, then roll out on a lightly floured surface and use to line a tart pan or to top a pie.

For flavor variations, try adding 1 teaspoon dry English mustard, a few chopped fresh herbs, or ½ cup freshly grated Parmesan or sharp cheddar cheese.

For sweet basic flaky pastry dough, add ¼ cup superfine sugar to the bowl with the flour and salt and use ¼ lb (1 stick) butter instead of a mixture of butter and shortening or lard. Continue as above.

For 12 double-crust, mini muffin-size pies or 6 double-crust 4 inch pies, make up the dough using 3 cups all-purpose flour, a pinch of salt, 6 tablespoons butter and ⅓ cup shortening or lard, or ¼ lb plus 4 tablespoons (1½ sticks) butter, and about ¼ cup cold water. For sweet pies, add ⅓ cup superfine sugar and all butter, not a mixture of fats.

To make 24 mini, muffin-size tart shells, use 1⅓ cups plus 1 tablespoon all-purpose flour, 6 tablespoons butter (or 3 tablespoons each of butter and shortening or lard), and 2 tablespoons cold water.

Pâte sucrée dough

This French-style dough is richer than the basic pie dough because it contains egg yolk. It is traditionally made straight on the work surface by mounding up the flour, then making a dip in the center. Add the sugar, soft butter, and egg yolks to the center, then work with your fingertips, drawing in more of the flour until it is all incorporated into a soft dough. Using a food processor, electric mixer, or bowl is much easier and less messy.

Makes 12 oz
Enough to make:
- A 9½ inch tart
- Or an 8 inch tart that is
  2 inches deep
- Or 12 muffin-size tarts
- Or 24 mini muffin-size tart shells

1⅓ cups **all-purpose flour**
⅓ cup **confectioner' sugar**
7 tablespoons **butter**, diced
2 **egg yolks**

Add the flour, confectioners' sugar, and butter to a food processor or mixing bowl and mix until you have fine crumbs. Add the egg yolks and mix together until you have a soft ball. Wrap in plastic wrap and chill for 15 minutes before using.
For flavor variations, add the grated rind of 1 small orange or 1 lemon, or 1 teaspoon ground cinnamon; or substitute 1 tablespoon of flour for 3 tablespoons unsweetened cocoa powder, sifted; or add ⅓ cup finely chopped hazelnuts with the egg yolks.

Hot water crust pastry dough

This traditional British dough is made in a completely different way by warming lard in milk, then mixing it into flour. When it has cooled, it can be pressed into a pan or molded over a greased jar or pie plate and chilled until set, then filled, topped with a pastry lid, and baked. It is a much more robust pastry that doesn't require such a light touch.

Makes 1½ lb
Enough to make:
- Six individual pies
- Or one large round 7 inch pie

¾ cup plus 2 tablespoons **lard**
¾ cup **milk**, or half milk and half water
3 cups **all-purpose flour**
¼ teaspoon **salt**

Add the lard and milk (or milk and water mix) to a saucepan and heat gently until the lard has just melted. Bring just to a boil, then transfer to a bowl containing the flour and salt and mix with a wooden spoon until it forms a smooth, soft ball.
Cover the top of the bowl with a clean cloth and let stand until cool enough to handle (about 10–20 minutes).
Knead lightly, then shape and bake according to the chosen recipe.
For flavor variations, try adding ¼ teaspoon cayenne pepper or 1 teaspoon English mustard powder when adding the flour and salt; or for a sweet version, add ¼ cup superfine sugar when heating the lard and milk.

Gluten-free pastry

If you have an intolerance to gluten, rice flour or wheat-free bread flour can be used instead of wheat flour. Unlike with wheat flour, the dough will be crumbly, so it requires careful handling; it can either be rolled out between two sheets of plastic wrap or pressed directly into a greased pan. If the dough does crack, simply press it back together again or patch with extra pieces of dough, sticking in place with beaten egg, milk, or water.

Makes 11 oz
Enough to make:
- Six 4 inch tart pans
- Or line a 9½ inch tart pan
- Or to cover four 1¼ cup individual pie plates
- Or a 1¼ quart pie plate

1⅓ cup **rice flour**
pinch of **salt**
7 tablespoons **butter**, diced
2 **egg yolks**
2 teaspoons **cold water**

Add the rice flour, salt, and butter to a mixing bowl and rub in with your fingertips or an electric mixer until you have fine crumbs. Add the egg yolks and mix to a soft dough, adding the water as required.
Roll out between two pieces of plastic wrap or press into a greased tart pan as required (see page 14).
For sweet gluten-free pastry, add ⅓ cup confections' sugar to the flour.

Cheat with prepared pastry

Puff pastry and phyllo pastry are so good that it is really not worth making your own. Keep a handy supply in the freezer, and remember to take it out in plenty of time so that the pastry can defrost at room temperature. When using puff pastry, try to keep an even pressure when rolling out so that the finished pie will rise evenly. Dust the surface very lightly with flour—just enough that it won't stick but not so much that the pastry becomes dry. Phyllo pastry can dry out quickly because the sheets are wafer thin. If shaping tiny boureks, unfold the pastry, but keep the remaining stack covered with plastic wrap or a dish cloth and try to use as quickly as possible.

If you are short on time, you may prefer to use store-bought piecrusts, which are perfectly acceptable alternatives to homemade ones.

Tips & techniques

Lining a tart pan

A loose-bottom tart pan makes it easy to remove the finished tart after baking.

Roll out the dough a little larger than the pan on a lightly floured surface. Lift over a rolling pin and drape into the pan.

Press over the bottom and up the sides of the pan with your fingertips, being careful at the bottom corner.

Trim off the excess dough with a knife just above the top of the pan to allow for shrinkage before or after baking.

14

Baking blind

This unusual term refers to baking the pastry shell while it is empty, so the filling doesn't make it soggy.

Prick the bottom of the pastry shell with a fork. Chill for 15 minutes to let the dough "relax"; this will help to minimize shrinkage during baking.

Line the tart pan with a piece of crumpled wax paper or nonstick parchment paper that is large enough to cover the bottom and sides of the pastry. Add a generous layer of pie weights—available from the cookware department of large department stores and speciality cookware shops—or improvise and use some dried beans, pasta, or rice.

Put the tart pan on a baking sheet and bake in a preheated oven, at 375°F, for 10–15 minutes for a large tart, 8–10 minutes for individual pastries, and 5 minutes for mini muffin-size pastries, until the shell is just set, then carefully lift the paper and weights out of the pastry shell and cook empty for 5 minutes for a large pastry, 4–5 minutes for individual pastries, and 2–3 minutes for mini muffin-size pastries until the bottom is dry and crisp and the top edges are pale golden.

Covering and decorating a pie

For a professional finish to a puff- or flaky pastry-topped meat or fruit pie.

Cut a narrow strip of pastry from the edges of the rolled-out dough, the same width as the rim of the pie plate. Brush the rim with water, beaten egg, or milk and stick the pastry strips in place, butting the ends of the strips together until the rim is completely covered.

Brush the strips with water, egg, or milk once again, then lift the remaining pastry over a rolling pin and drape over the top of the pie. Press the edges together to create a seal, then trim off the excess pastry with a small knife.

Press up the edges of the pie by making small horizontal cuts around the edge of the pastry rim. This helps to encourage the puff pastry layers to separate and rise during baking and can also give the impression of layers in a basic flaky pastry pie.

Flute the edges by pressing the first and second finger onto the pie edge, then make small cuts with a knife between them to create a scalloped edge. Repeat all the way around the pie. Brush the pie with a little beaten or milk to glaze it.

To decorate with pastry leaves, reroll the pastry trimmings if needed and cut a strip about 1 inch wide, then cut out diamond shapes. Mark veins with the knife, then curl the ends of the leaf and position on the glazed pie. Glaze the decoration with beaten egg or milk. Alternatively, hearts, circles, festive shapes, or numbers can be stamped from rerolled pastry trimmings with small cookie cutters, then arranged on the glazed pie and glazed with a little more beaten egg or milk. For smaller pies, it can also be effective to stamp out small holes with cutters so that the filling can be seen.

bite-size
snacks

pissaldiere bites

Makes **18**
Preparation time **25 minutes**
Cooking time **25–30 minutes**

2 tablespoons **olive oil**, plus
   extra to serve (optional)
2 **onions**, thinly sliced
1 **garlic clove**, finely chopped
1 teaspoon **superfine sugar**
small bunch of **thyme**
8 oz **store-bought puff
   pastry**, defrosted if frozen
1 **beaten egg**, to glaze
9 **anchovy fillets** from a can,
   drained
9 small **stuffed green olives**
salt and **pepper**

Heat the oil in a skillet, add the onions, and sauté gently for 10 minutes, until soft and just beginning to color. Add the garlic and sugar and sauté for another 5 minutes, until golden. Take the skillet off the heat, tear leaves from half the thyme and sprinkle over the onion, and season with salt and pepper.

Roll the pastry out on a lightly floured surface and trim to a 6 × 12 inch rectangle, then cut into 2 inch squares. Transfer the squares to an oiled baking sheet, leaving a little space between them.

Brush the tops with beaten egg, then divide the onion mixture among them. Cut each anchovy fillet into 2 thin strips and arrange 2 on each pastry square as a cross, then top with a halved olive.

Bake in a preheated oven, at 400°F, for 10–15 minutes, until the pastry is well risen and golden. Brush the olives with a little extra oil, if liked, and sprinkle with the remaining thyme leaves. Serve warm or cold with drinks.

For feta & red pepper bites, top the pastry squares with a mixture of 1 thinly sliced onion sautéed in 1 tablespoon olive oil until golden, 1 finely chopped garlic clove, ¾ cup drained and sliced roasted red peppers (from a jar), ¾ cup crumbled feta cheese, a few thyme leaves, and salt and pepper. Bake as above.

spinach boureks

Makes **36**
Preparation time **30 minutes**
Cooking time **15 minutes**

2½ cups barely defrosted
  frozen spinach
1 cup **cream cheese**
2 **garlic cloves**, finely
  chopped
1 **egg**, beaten
a little **grated nutmeg**
6 sheets **phyllo pastry**,
  19 × 9 inches, defrosted
  if frozen
¼ lb (1 stick) **butter**, melted
salt and **pepper**

Add the spinach to a strainer set over a bowl and press out the juices with the back of a spoon. In another bowl, mix together the cream cheese, garlic, and egg. Stir in the spinach and season with nutmeg, salt, and pepper.

Unfold the pastry sheets and put one sheet on the work surface with the long edge facing you. Cover the remaining sheets with plastic wrap so that they don't dry out. Brush the pastry in front of you with a little melted butter, then cut into six 3 × 9 inch strips. Put a teaspoon of the spinach mixture near the bottom right corner of each strip.

Holding the bottom right corner of one of the strips, lift and fold up and over diagonally to make a triangular shape to enclose the filling. Fold the bottom left corner straight upward to make a thicker triangle, then continue folding until you reach the top of the pastry.

Make 5 more boureks, then take a second sheet of pastry and repeat. Continue until all the pastry and filling has been used. Transfer to a baking sheet and brush with the remaining butter. Bake in a preheated oven, at 350°F, for 15 minutes, until golden. Let cool slightly, then serve warm or cold.

For eggplant boureks, sauté 1 chopped onion and 1 diced eggplant in 2 tablespoons olive oil until softened. Add 2 finely chopped garlic cloves and 1 (14½ oz) can diced tomatoes, 1 teaspoon superfine sugar, ¼ teaspoon ground allspice, and salt and pepper. Cover and simmer for 15–20 minutes, until the eggplant is soft. Let cool, then make up the boureks with pastry and butter and cook as above.

mini harissa sausage rolls

Makes **30**
Preparation time **30 minutes**
Cooking time **20 minutes**

1 lb good-quality **bulk
sausage** or **sausage meat**
removed from its casings
⅓ cup coarsely chopped
walnut pieces
2 inch piece **fresh ginger
root**, peeled and coarsely
grated
1 teaspoon **black
peppercorns**, coarsely
crushed
16 oz **store-bought puff
pastry**, defrosted if frozen
beaten egg, to glaze
3 teaspoons **harissa paste**
salt

Add the bulk sausage meat, walnuts, and ginger to a
large bowl, sprinkle with the pepper and a little salt,
then mix together with a wooden spoon or your hands.

Roll the pastry out thinly on a lightly floured surface
and trim to a 12 inch square. Cut the square into
3 strips, 4 inches wide, then brush lightly with beaten
egg. Spread 1 teaspoon of harissa in a band down the
center of each pastry strip, then top each strip with
one-third of the sausage meat mixture, spooning into
a narrow band.

Fold the pastry over the filling and press the edges
together well with the flattened tip of a small, sharp
knife. Trim the edge to tidy, if needed, then slash
the top of the strips.

Brush the sausage rolls with beaten egg, then cut
each strip into 10 pieces and arrange slightly spaced
apart on 2 lightly oiled baking sheets. Cook in a
preheated oven, at 400°F, for about 20 minutes, until
golden and the pastry is well risen. Transfer to a wire
rack, then let cool for 20 minutes. Serve warm or cold.

For curried sausage rolls, omit the walnuts from
the sausage meat filling, adding ⅓ cup golden raisins,
1 teaspoon turmeric, 2 chopped garlic cloves, and
2 tablespoons chopped cilantro. Spread each pastry
strip with 1 teaspoon mild curry paste, then top with
the sausage meat mixture, shape, and bake as above.

mini phyllo & guacamole cups

Makes **16**
Preparation time **30 minutes**
Cooking time **4–5 minutes**

1 sheet of **phyllo pastry**,
   19 × 9 inches, defrosted
   if frozen
2 tablespoons **butter**, melted
1 ripe **avocado**
juice of **1 lime**
½ mild **red chile**, seeded
   and finely chopped, plus
   extra to garnish
1 **scallion**, finely chopped
2 tablespoons finely chopped
   cilantro, plus extra to garnish
salt and **pepper**

Unfold the pastry sheet, brush with butter, then cut into 32 small squares about 2 inches each. Gently press 1 square into 16 cups of two 12-cup mini muffin pans, then add a second square of pastry to each at right angles to the first for a petal-like effect.

Bake in a preheated oven, at 375°F, for 4–5 minutes, until golden. Lift the phyllo cups out of the pans and cool on a wire rack.

Halve, pit, and peel the avocado, then mash with the lime juice or process in a food processor. Add the chile, scallion, and cilantro, season lightly with salt and pepper, and mix together.

Spoon the guacamole into the phyllo cups, garnish with extra chopped chile and cilantro, if liked, and serve within 1 hour of finishing because the avocado will discolor.

For mini phyllo & taramasalata cups, make the cups as above, then fill with ½ (14 oz) jar of chilled taramasalata and garnish with a few chopped ripe black olives and a little chopped parsley.

parmesan & tomato tarts

Makes **24**
Preparation time **30 minutes**,
  plus chilling
Cooking time **18–20 minutes**

2 **eggs**
⅓ cup **milk**
½ cup finely grated **Parmesan cheese**
3 **scallions**, finely chopped
8 small **cherry tomatoes**,
  thickly sliced
salt and **pepper**
tiny **basil leaves**, to garnish

For the pastry
1⅓ cups plus 1 tablespoon
  all-purpose flour
6 tablespoons **butter**, diced
2 tablespoons chopped **basil**
2 tablespoons **cold water**

Make the pastry. Add the flour, a little salt and pepper, and the butter to a mixing bowl, then rub in the butter with your fingertips or using an electric mixer until you have fine crumbs. Add the basil, then mix in enough water to form a soft but not sticky dough.

Knead the pastry lightly, then roll it out thinly on a lightly floured surface. Stamp out twenty-four 2½ inch circles with a plain cookie cutter, then press into the buttered cups of two 12-cup mini muffin pans, rerolling the trimmings as needed. Chill for 15 minutes.

Beat together the eggs and milk in a bowl. Add the Parmesan, scallions, and a little salt and pepper and mix well. Spoon into the tarts, then add a slice of tomato to each one.

Bake in a preheated oven, at 350°F, for 18–20 minutes, until golden and the filling is just set. Let stand for 10 minutes, then loosen the edges of the tarts and remove from the pans. Garnish with tiny basil leaves just before serving.

For Parmesan & shrimp tarts, omit the sliced tomatoes from the tarts and add 1 small, cooked peeled shrimp, defrosted if frozen, to each instead. Bake as above.

medieval spiced steak pies

Makes **24**

Preparation time **30 minutes**, plus chilling

Cooking time **15 minutes**

1 quantity **basic flaky pastry dough** (see page 9)

beaten egg, to glaze

sifted **confectioners' sugar**, for dusting

For the filling

½ cup **brandy**

⅔ cup **dried currants**

⅔ cup **raisins**

2 tablespoons chopped **crystallized** or **preserved ginger**

grated rind of ½ **orange**

grated rind of ½ **lemon**

½ teaspoon **ground allspice**

¼ teaspoon **grated nutmeg**

⅓ cup **blanched almonds**, chopped

8 oz **extra lean ground beef**

½ cup **shredded suet** or **shortening**

1 **tart apple**, cored and grated

Make the filling. Pour the brandy into a saucepan, bring just to a boil, then add the dried fruits, ginger, fruit rinds, and spices and let cool. Mix in the almonds, beef, suet, and apple, then cover and let stand in the refrigerator overnight so that the flavors can develop.

Next day, roll out two-thirds of the dough on a lightly floured surface and stamp out 3 inch circles with a plain cookie cutter. Press into the buttered cups of two 12-cup muffin pans, rerolling the dough as needed. Spoon in the filling.

Add any trimmings to the reserved dough, then roll out and stamp out twenty-four 2½ inch plain circles for the pie tops, rerolling the trimmings as needed. Brush the edges of the filled pies with beaten egg, add the lids, and press the edges together well.

Brush the tops with beaten egg, then make 4 small steam vents. Bake in a preheated oven, at 375°F, for 15 minutes, until the pastry is golden. let stand for 10 minutes, then loosen the edges of the pastry and transfer to a wire rack to cool. Just before serving, dust the tops lightly with sifted confectioners' sugar. These are delicious served as an appetizer before the Christmas roasted turkey or a special dinner.

For traditional dessert mince pies, omit the ground beef and add 1 cup golden raisins and ⅓ cup firmly packed light brown sugar. Continue as above.

feta & scallion cigarellos

Makes **18**
Preparation time **25 minutes**
Cooking time **10–12 minutes**

1⅓ cups drained, crumbled
  feta cheese
3 **scallions**, finely chopped
3 tablespoons **Greek yogurt**
1 **egg**, beaten
3 sheets of **phyllo pastry**,
  19 × 9 inches, defrosted
  if frozen
4 tablespoons **butter**, melted
3 tablespoons **sesame
  seeds**, for sprinkling
  (optional)
pepper

Beat the feta, onions, yogurt, and egg together and
season with a little pepper. Spoon into a pastry bag
fitted with a large plain tip.

Unfold the pastry sheets and put one sheet on your
work surface with the long edge facing you. Brush with
a little of the butter, then cut into 3 strips, 6 × 9 inches,
then cut in half to make 6 × 4½ inch rectangles.

Pipe a line of the feta cheese mixture about 1 inch
from the long side of each rectangle and a little in from
the short sides. Fold the short sides in, then the bottom
of the pastry, and roll up to completely enclose the
filling and make a thin cigarlike shape. Continue until
you have 6 cigarellos from the sheet of pastry.

Repeat with the remaining pastry sheets and feta
mixture. Arrange on an ungreased baking sheet and
brush the outside of each with the remaining butter.
Sprinkle with a few sesame seeds, if liked. Bake in a
preheated oven, at 375°F, for 10–12 minutes, until the
pastry is golden brown.

Let cool, then serve while still warm with salad as an
appetizer or glasses of chilled wine as an aperitif.

For pesto cigarellos, brush each pastry sheet with
a little melted butter, then spread thinly with red pesto
(you will need 3 tablespoons in total). Pipe on the feta
mixture and continue as above. Shape and brush with
the remaining butter and sprinkle with a few salt flakes
instead of the sesame seeds before baking.

samosas

Makes **18**
Preparation time **30 minutes**
Cooking time **35–45 minutes**

3 medium **baking potatoes**
    (about 10 oz), scrubbed but
    unpeeled
2 tablespoons **sunflower oil**,
1 **onion**, finely chopped
1½ teaspoons **black mustard
    seeds**
2 teaspoons **cumin seeds**,
    coarsely crushed
2 **Thai green chiles**, with
    seeds, finely chopped
1 teaspoon **coriander seeds**,
    crushed
3 tablespoons chopped
    cilantro
¼ teaspoon **turmeric**
½ cup **frozen peas**, defrosted
4 cups **sunflower oil**, for
    deep-frying
salt and **pepper**

For the dough
1⅔ cups **all-purpose flour**
4 tablespoons **butter** or **ghee**,
    diced
4–5 tablespoons **cold water**

Cook the potatoes in boiling water for 15–20 minutes,
until tender. Drain and let stand until cool enough to
handle, then peel off the skins and dice the flesh.

Heat the oil in the drained and dried potato saucepan,
add the onion, and sauté for 3 minutes, then add the
mustard seeds, cumin seeds, and chiles and cook for
2 minutes. Mix in the coriander, cilantro, and turmeric,
then the potatoes, peas, and plenty of salt and pepper.

Make the dough. Add the flour, a little salt, and the
butter or ghee to a mixing bowl, rub in the butter with
your fingertips until you have fine crumbs, then mix in
enough of the water to form a soft but not sticky dough.
Knead well until smooth and elastic. Cut into 9 pieces
and shape into balls. Roll out to 5 inch circles.

Cut each circle in half, brush the edges with water, then
shape into a cone by folding one point to the center of
the curved top; do the same with the other point. Spoon
the filling into the cone, then press the curved edges
together to seal. Repeat to make 18 samosas.

Fill a large saucepan halfway with oil, and heat to 350°F
on a sugar thermometer or until the oil bubbles when a
samosa is dropped into the oil. Cook the samosas in
batches of 3 or 4 for 3–4 minutes, until golden brown,
then lift out and transfer to a plate lined with paper
towels. Serve warm with mango chutney or raita.

For gingered shrimp samosas, reduce the amount
of potato to 2 (about 7 oz), cook as above, then add
1 inch piece fresh ginger root, peeled and grated,
along with the chiles. Mix in 4 oz small cooked, peeled
shrimp, defrosted if frozen, with the peas.

papaya, lime & mango tarts

Makes **20**

Preparation time **35 minutes**, plus chilling

Cooking time **15–20 minutes**

8 oz chilled store-bought or homemade **sweet basic flaky pastry dough** (see page 10) or **pâte sucrée dough** (see page 11)

thinly grated rind and juice of 2 large, juicy **limes**

⅓ cup **heavy cream**

⅔ cup **condensed milk**

2 tablespoons finely diced **mango**

2 tablespoons finely diced **papaya**

lime rind, to decorate

Roll the dough out on a lightly floured surface to ⅛ inch thickness, then, stamp out twenty 2 inch circles using a plain cookie cutter. Use the circles to line twenty 2 inch mini tart pans. Prick the pastry bottoms with a fork. Chill. Line the tarts with squares of nonstick parchment paper and pie weights or dried beans and bake in a preheated oven, at 375°F, for 10 minutes, then remove the paper and weights and return the pastry shells to the oven for 8–10 minutes, until they are crisp and golden. Remove the shells from the pan and cool on a wire rack.

Put the lime rind in a blender with the cream and condensed milk and process until well combined. With the motor running, slowly pour in the lime juice and process until blended. (Alternatively, mix well by hand.) Transfer to a bowl, cover, and chill for 3–4 hours, until firm.

Put the pastry shells on a serving platter and spoon the lime mixture evenly among the shells. Mix the mango with the papaya and, using a teaspoon, fill the shells. Decorate with lime rind and serve immediately.

For blueberry & raspberry tarts, make the pastry shells and filling as above. Spoon the lime mixture into the shells. Warm 3 tablespoons grape jelly with the grated rind and juice of 1 lime, cook until syrupy, then stir in 1 cup blueberries and 1¼ cups raspberries. Spoon over the top of the tarts.

mini chocolate truffle tarts

Makes **24**

Preparation time **30 minutes**, plus chilling

Cooking time **9–10 minutes**

1 quantity **pâte sucrée dough** (see page 11), chilled

1 cup **heavy cream**

2 tablespoons **confectioners' sugar**

8 oz **semisweet dark chocolate**, broken into pieces

¼ cup **brandy**

chocolate curls, to decorate

sifted **confectioners' sugar**, for dusting (optional)

Roll the dough out thinly on a lightly floured surface, then stamp out twenty-four 2½ inch circles with a fluted cookie cutter and press into the buttered cups of two 12-cup mini muffin pans. Reknead and reroll the dough trimmings as needed. Prick the bottom of each tart 2–3 times with a fork, then chill for 15 minutes.

Line the tarts with small squares of nonstick parchment paper and pie weights or dried beans and bake in a preheated oven, at 375°F, for 5 minutes. Remove the paper and weights and cook for another 4–5 minutes, until the bottoms are crisp. Remove the shells from the pans and cool on a wire rack.

Pour the cream into a small saucepan, add the sugar, and bring just to a boil. Remove from the heat, add the chocolate, and let stand for 5 minutes, until melted. Stir until smooth, then gradually mix in the brandy. Let cool, then transfer to the refrigerator for about 1 hour, until thick enough to pipe.

Spoon the mixture into a pastry bag fitted with a star tip and pipe whirls of truffle mixture into each tart shell. Decorate with chocolate curls, made using a swivel vegetable peeler, dust with a little sifted confectioners' sugar, if liked, and chill until ready to serve.

For chiled chocolate truffle tarts, instead of plain semsiweet dark chocolate, melt 8 oz of semisweet dark chocolate with chile bars in the cream, then add ¼ cup rum instead of brandy. Chill, then pipe into the baked tarts as above.

baby banana & peach strudels

Makes **8**
Preparation time **30 minutes**
Cooking time **15–18 minutes**

2 **bananas** (about 12 oz),
  peeled and chopped
2 tablespoons **lemon juice**
2 small **ripe peaches** (about
  7 oz), halved, pitted, and
  sliced
²⁄₃ cup **blueberries**
2 tablespoons **superfine
  sugar**
2 tablespoons **fresh bread
  crumbs**
½ teaspoon **ground
  cinnamo**n
6 sheets of **phyllo pastry**,
  each 19 x 9 inches,
  defrosted if frozen
4 tablespoons **butter**, melted
sifted **confectioners' sugar**,
  for dusting

Toss the bananas in the lemon juice, then place in a
large bowl with the peach slices and blueberries. Mix
the sugar, bread crumbs, and cinnamon in a small bowl,
then gently mix with the fruit.

Unfold the pastry sheets and put one sheet on your
work surface with the long edge facing you. Cut in half
to make two 9 x 10 inch rectangles. Put 2 heaping
spoonfuls of the fruit mixture on each, then fold in the
sides, brush the pastry with a little of the melted butter,
and roll up like a package. Repeat to make 8 mini
strudels using 4 sheets of pastry.

Brush the strudels with a little more melted butter. Cut
the remaining pastry sheets into wide strips, then wrap
them like bandages around the strudels, covering any
tears or splits in the pastry. Place on an ungreased
baking sheet and brush with the remaining butter.

Bake the strudels in a preheated oven, at 375°F, for
15–18 minutes, until golden brown and crisp. Let cool
on the baking sheet, then dust with a little sifted
confectioners' sugar and arrange on a serving plate.
These are best eaten on the day they are made.

For traditional apple strudels, replace the bananas
and peaches with 2 large cooking apples (about 1 lb)
cored, peeled, and sliced, tossed with 2 tablespoons
lemon juice, and mixed with ⅓ cup golden raisins.
Replace the bread crumbs with 2 tablespoons ground
almonds and combine with the cinnamon. Increase
the quantity of sugar to ¼ cup and continue the recipe
as above.

40

lemon curd tarts

Makes **24**
Preparation time **40 minutes**,
 plus chilling and cooling
Cooking time **15 minutes**

1 quantity **pâte sucrée dough**
 (see page 11), chilled
2 **eggs**
1 cup **superfine sugar**
4 tablespoons **butter**, melted
grated rind of 1½ **lemons**,
 plus extra to decorate
¼ cup **lemon juice**
¾ cup **crème fraîche**

Roll the dough out thinly on a lightly floured surface, then stamp out twenty-four 2½ inch circles with a fluted cookie cutter and press into the buttered cups of two 12-cup mini muffin pans. Reknead and reroll the dough trimmings as needed. Prick the bottom of each tart 2–3 times with a fork, then chill for 15 minutes.

Beat the eggs and sugar together, then mix in the melted butter, lemon rind, and lemon juice. Spoon into the tart shells and bake in a preheated oven, at 350°F, for 15 minutes, until just set. The tarts will be puffed up when you first take them out of the oven, but as they cool they will sink down again.

Let cool in the pans, then loosen the pastry with a knife, lift the tarts out of the pans, and arrange on a serving plate. Top each with a small spoonful of crème fraîche and grated lemon rind to garnish.

For citrus curd tarts, make the filling with the grated rind of ½ lemon, ½ lime, and ½ orange and ¼ cup of mixed juice. Continue as above.

white chocolate & raspberry tarts

Makes **24**
Preparation time **30 minutes**,
  plus chilling and cooling
Cooking time **9–10 minutes**

1 quantity **pâte sucrée dough**
  (see page 11), chilled
5 oz **white chocolate**, broken
  into pieces
1¼ cups **heavy cream**
2 tablespoons finely chopped
  mint
24 **raspberries**
tiny **mint leaves**, to decorate
sifted **confectioners' sugar**,
  for dusting

Roll the dough out thinly on a lightly floured surface, then stamp out twenty-four 2½ inch circles with a fluted cookie cutter and press into the buttered cups of two 12-cup mini muffin pans. Reknead and reroll the pastry trimmings as needed. Prick the bottom of each tart 2–3 times with a fork, then chill for 15 minutes.

Line the tarts with small squares of nonstick parchment paper and pie weights or dried beans and bake in a preheated oven, at 375°F, for 5 minutes. Remove the paper and weights and cook for another 4–5 minutes, until the bottoms are crisp. Remove the shells from the pans and cool on a wire rack.

Melt the chocolate in a bowl over a saucepan of gently simmering water, making sure that the bottom of the bowl does not touch the water. Stir until smooth.

Whip the cream until it forms soft swirls, then fold in the melted chocolate and chopped mint. Spoon into the cooled pastry shells and top each one with a raspberry and tiny mint leaf. Dust lightly with sifted confectioners' sugar just before serving.

For dark chocolate & raspberry tarts, make the pastry dough, replacing 2 tablespoons of the flour with 3 tablespoons unsweetened cocoa powder. Fold 4 oz melted semisweet dark chocolate into the cream with 2 tablespoons confectioners' sugar and the finely chopped mint. Decorate with raspberries, tiny mint leaves, and a dusting of sifted confectioners' sugar as above.

citrus baklava

Makes **24**
Preparation time **30 minutes**,
  plus chilling
Cooking time **35–40 minutes**

13 oz **phyllo pastry**, defrosted
  if frozen
¼ lb (1 stick) **butter**, melted

For the filling
¾ cup **walnut pieces**
¾ cup **shelled pistachio nuts**
⅔ cup **blanched almonds**
⅓ cup **superfine sugar**
½ teaspoon **ground cinnamon**

For the syrup
1 **lemon**
1 small **orange**
2¼ cups **superfine sugar**
pinch of **ground cinnamon**
⅔ cup **water**

To decorate
few slivers **pistachio nuts**

Make the filling. Dry-fry the nuts in a nonstick saucepan for 3–4 minutes, stirring until lightly browned. let cool slightly, then coarsely chop and mix with the sugar and spice.

Unfold the pastry and cut it into rectangles the same size as the bottom of a small 7 x 11 inch baking pan. Wrap half the pastry in plastic wrap so that it doesn't dry out. Brush each unwrapped sheet of pastry with melted butter, then layer in the baking pan. Spoon in the nut mixture, then unwrap and cover with the remaining pastry, buttering the layers as you work.

Cut the pastry into 6 squares, then cut each square into 4 triangles. Bake in a preheated oven, at 350°F, for 30–35 minutes, covering with aluminum foil after 20 minutes to prevent them from overbrowning.

Meanwhile, make the syrup. Pare the rind off the citrus fruits with a zester or vegetable peeler, then cut the rind into strips. Squeeze the juice. Put the strips and juice in a saucepan with the sugar, cinnamon, and water. Heat gently until the sugar dissolves, then simmer for 5 minutes without stirring.

Pour the hot syrup over the pastry as soon as it comes out of the oven. Let cool, then chill for 3 hours. Remove from the pan and arrange the pieces on a serving plate, sprinkled with slivers of pistachio. Store in the refrigerator for up to 2 days.

For rose water baklava, omit the orange rind and juice from the syrup and add ¼ cup extra water and 1 tablespoon rose water, or to taste. Pour over the cooked baklava and finish as above.

mini pine nut & honey tarts

Makes **24**

Preparation time **30 minutes**,
   plus chilling

Cooking time **17–20 minutes**

1 quantity **pâte sucrée dough**
   (see page 11), chilled
4 tablespoons **butter**, at room
   temperature
¼ cup **superfine sugar**
3 tablespoons **thick honey**
grated rind of ½ **lemon**
1 **egg**
1 **egg yolk**
¾ cup **pine nuts**
sifted **confectioners' sugar**,
   for dusting (optional)

Roll the dough out thinly on a lightly floured surface,
then stamp out twenty-four 2½ inch circles with
a fluted cookie cutter and press into the buttered cups
of two 12-cup mini muffin pans. Reknead and reroll the
dough trimmings as needed. Prick the bottom of each
tart 2–3 times with a fork, then chill for 15 minutes.

Line the tarts with small squares of nonstick parchment
paper and pie weights or dried beans and bake in a
preheated oven, at 375°F, for 5 minutes. Remove the
paper and weights and cook for another 4–5 minutes,
until the bottoms are crisp.

Cream the butter and sugar together, beat in the
honey and lemon rind, then the egg and egg yolk.
Reserve about one-quarter of the pine nuts, then stir
the rest into the honey mix.

Spoon into the baked pastry shells and sprinkle with
the remaining pine nuts. Bake for 8–10 minutes, until
golden and the filling is set. Let cool for 15 minutes,
then remove from the pans and let cool on a wire rack.
Dust with confectioners' sugar, if liked.

For spiced walnut & honey tarts, make the pastry
shells and filling as above, replacing the lemon rind
and pine nuts with ¼ teaspoon ground cinnamon and
¾ cup chopped walnuts.

blueberry tarts

Makes **24**
Preparation time **30 minutes**,
   plus chilling and cooling
Cooking time **11–13 minutes**

1 quantity of **orange-flavored
   pâte sucrée dough** (see
   page 11), chilled
2 teaspoons **cornstarch**
3 teaspoons **water**
3 tablespoons **superfine
   sugar**, plus extra for
   sprinkling
2 cups **blueberries**
milk, to glaze

Roll the pastry out thinly on a lightly floured surface,
then stamp out twenty-four 2½ inch circles with a
fluted cookie cutter and press into the buttered cups of
two 12-cup mini muffin pans, reserving any trimmings.
Prick the bottom of each tart 2–3 times with a fork,
then chill for 15 minutes.

Meanwhile, mix the cornstarch and measured water to
a paste in a saucepan, then add the sugar and half the
blueberries. Cook over medium heat for 2–3 minutes,
until the blueberries soften and the juices begin to
run. Remove from the heat and add the remaining
blueberries. Let cool.

Roll out the remaining dough trimmings and cut out
24 tiny heart shapes. Place the hearts on a baking
sheet, brush with milk, and sprinkle with superfine sugar.

Line the tarts with small squares of nonstick parchment
paper and pie weights or dried beans and bake in a
preheated oven, at 375°F, for 5 minutes. Remove the
paper and weights from the tarts and cook for another
4–5 minutes, until the bottoms are crisp, cooking the
hearts for 4–5 minutes on the shelf below.

Transfer the tart shells to a wire rack to cool. When
ready to serve, spoon in the blueberry compote and top
with the hearts.

For mini jam tarts, make the tart shells and pastry
shapes as above. Spoon in ⅔ cup strawberry jam,
add the pastry shapes, then bake in a preheated
oven, at 350°F, for 12–15 minutes. Let the tarts
cool for 5 minutes, then transfer to a wire rack
to cool completely.

plum tripiti

Makes **24**
Preparation time **40 minutes**
Cooking time **10 minutes**

$\frac{2}{3}$ cup drained, crumbled
feta cheese
$\frac{1}{3}$ cup **ricotta cheese**
$\frac{1}{4}$ cup **superfine sugar**
$\frac{1}{4}$ teaspoon **ground cinnamon**
1 **egg**, beaten
6 tablespoons **unsalted
butter**
12 sheets chilled **phyllo
pastry**
a little **flour**, for dusting
8 small red **plums** (about
1 lb), halved and pitted
confectioners' sugar, for
dusting

Mix the feta, ricotta, sugar, cinnamon, and egg in a
bowl. Melt the butter in a small saucepan.

Unfold the pastry sheets on a lightly floured surface,
then put one in front of you, with a short side facing
you. Cover the remaining sheets with plastic wrap to
prevent them from drying out. Brush the pastry sheet
with a little of the melted butter, then cut in half to
make two long strips. Place a spoonful of the cheese
mixture a little up from the bottom left-hand corner of
each strip, then cover with a plum half. Fold the bottom
right-hand corner of one strip diagonally over the plum
to cover the filling and to make a triangle.

Fold the bottom left-hand corner upward to make a
second triangle, then keep folding until the top of the
strip is reached and the filling is enclosed in a triangle
of pastry. Place on a baking sheet and repeat until
24 triangles have been made using all the filling.

Brush the outside of the triangles with the remaining
butter and cook in a preheated oven, at 400°F, for
about 10 minutes, until the pastry is golden and the
plum juices begin to run from the sides. Dust with
a little sifted confectioners' sugar and let cool for
15 minutes before serving.

For gingered peach tripiti, make the filling in the
same way but flavor with 2 tablespoons finely
chopped crystallized or preserved ginger instead of
ground cinnamon. Top with 2 ripe peaches, each cut
into 12 pieces.

english treacle tarts

Makes **24**

Preparation time **30 minutes**,
  plus chilling

Cooking time **25 minutes**

1 quantity **pâte sucrée dough**
  (see page 11), chilled
4 tablespoons **butter**
1/3 cup firmly packed **light
  brown sugar**
1 1/4 cups **golden syrup** or
  light corn syrup
grated rind of 1 **lemon**
2 tablespoons **lemon juice**
1 **egg**, beaten
1 cup **fresh bread crumbs**

Roll the dough out thinly on a lightly floured surface,
then stamp out twenty-four 2 1/2 inch circles with a
fluted cookie cutter and press into the buttered cups of
two 12-cup mini muffin pans. Reknead and reroll pastry
trimmings as needed. Chill for 15 minutes.

Put the butter, sugar, syrup, lemon rind, and lemon juice
in a small saucepan and cook over low heat until the
butter has just melted and the sugar dissolved. Remove
from the heat and let cool slightly.

Stir the beaten egg and bread crumbs into the syrup
mix and beat until smooth. Spoon into the pastry shells.

Bake the tarts in a preheated oven, at 350°F, for
15–20 minutes. Let cool for 15 minutes, then loosen
the tarts with a knife and remove from the pans.
Transfer to a wire rack and let cool slightly. Serve
warm with spoonfuls of whipped cream sprinkled
with ground cinnamon.

For ginger & oat treacle tarts, add 1 teaspoon
ground ginger to the syrup mix, then stir in the lemon
rind and juice, beaten egg, and 1/2 cup rolled oats
instead of the bread crumbs. Cook as above.

portuguese custard tarts

Makes **12**

Preparation time **25 minutes**,
   plus cooling

Cooking time **35 minutes**

1 tablespoon **vanilla sugar**

½ teaspoon **ground cinnamon**

14½ oz chilled store-bought or
   homemade **sweet basic
   flaky pastry pastry** (see
   page 10)

a little **flour**, for dusting

3 **eggs**

2 **egg yolks**

2 tablespoons **superfine
   sugar**

1 teaspoon **vanilla extract**

1¼ cups **heavy cream**

⅔ cup **milk**

confectioners' sugar, for
   dusting

Mix the vanilla sugar with the cinnamon. Cut the pastry in half and roll out each piece on a lightly floured surface to an 8 inch square. Sprinkle 1 square with the spiced sugar and position the second square on top. Reroll the pastry to a 16 x 12 inch rectangle and cut out 12 circles, each 4 inches across, using a large cutter or small bowl as a guide.

Press the pastry circles into the cups of a 12-cup nonstick muffin pan, pressing them firmly into the bottom and around the sides. Prick each pastry bottom, line with a square of parchment paper, add pie weights or dried beans, and bake in a preheated oven, at 375°F, for 10 minutes. Remove the paper and weights and bake for an additional 5 minutes. Reduce the oven temperature to 325°F.

Beat together the eggs, egg yolks, superfine sugar, and vanilla extract. Heat the cream and milk in a saucepan until bubbling around the edges and pour it over the egg mixture, stirring. Strain the custard into a pitcher and pour into the pastry shells.

Bake for about 20 minutes or until the custard is only just set. Let the tarts cool in the pan, then remove and serve dusted with confectioners' sugar.

For French prune custard tarts, put 12 pitted prunes (dried plums) in the bottom of each baked pastry shell, then pour the custard over and bake as above. Serve warm with spoonfuls of crème fraîche.

savory
light bites

smoked salmon & mint pea tarts

Makes **6**
Preparation time **20 minutes**
Cooking time **15 minutes**

16 oz **store-bought puff pastry**, defrosted if frozen
2 tablespoons **butter**
6 **scallions**, thinly sliced
1¾ cups **frozen peas**, defrosted
2 **Boston lettuce**, thickly sliced
2 tablespoons chopped **mint**
1 cup **crème fraîche**
8 oz **smoked salmon**
salt and **pepper**

Cut the pastry into 6 pieces, then roll each piece out on a lightly floured surface and trim to a 6 inch circle using a saucer as a guide. Transfer to 2 large, lightly oiled baking sheets. Mark smaller circles 1 inch in from the edges, then prick all over the inner circles with a fork.

Bake in a preheated oven, at 400°F, for 10 minutes, until well risen. Press down the center with a fork and cook for another 5 minutes, until the tart shells are crisp and golden.

When the tart shells are almost ready, heat the butter in a skillet, then add the scallions and sauté until softened. Add the peas and cook for a few minutes until hot, add the lettuce, and cook for 30 seconds, then stir in the mint, crème fraîche, and salt and pepper.

Spoon the pea mixture into the hot tart shells and arrange the smoked salmon in folds on top. Sprinkle with a little extra pepper and serve immediately with a salad.

For bacon, pea & spinach tarts, make the tart shells as above. Sauté the scallions in butter, add the peas and 5 cups spinach, and cook until just wilted. Stir in the crème fraîche, 1 teaspoon whole-grain mustard, salt, and pepper, then spoon into the tart shells and top with 6 broiled and diced bacon slices.

mexican egg tarts

Makes **4**

Preparation time **25 minutes**, plus chilling

Cooking time **25–28 minutes**

1 quantity **basic flaky pastry dough** (see page 9)

1 tablespoon **olive oil**

1 **onion**, chopped

1 **red bell pepper**, cored, seeded, and diced

3 oz **chorizo sausage, diced**

2 **garlic cloves**, finely chopped

¼ teaspoon **smoked paprika**

2 **bay leaves**

¾ cup canned **diced tomatoes**

1 cup halved **cherry tomatoes**

4 **eggs**

salt and **pepper**

a few **tiny basil leaves**, optional

shredded **cheddar cheese**, to serve

Divide the dough into 4 pieces, then roll each piece out on a lightly floured surface until a little larger than a buttered, 5 inch loose-bottom fluted tart pan. Lift the dough into the pan, then press over the bottom and sides. Trim off the excess dough with scissors a little above the top of the pan. Prick the bottom with a fork, then put on a baking sheet. Chill for 15 minutes.

Heat the oil in a saucepan, add the onion, bell pepper, and chorizo, and sauté for 5 minutes, until softened. Stir in the garlic, paprika, and bay leaves, then add the canned tomatoes and season with salt and pepper. Simmer gently, uncovered, for 15 minutes, stirring from time to time until thickened. Discard the bay leaves.

Meanwhile, bake the tarts blind (see page 15) for 8 minutes. Remove the paper and weights and cook for another 4 minutes, until golden.

Stir the cherry tomatoes into the hot sauce and spoon into the hot pastry shells. Make a dip in the center, then break an egg into each. Sprinkle with salt and pepper and cook for 5–8 minutes until the egg is to your liking.

Remove the tarts from the pans, transfer to serving plates, sprinkle with basil leaves, if desired, shredded cheese, and serve with a three bean salad.

For creamy spinach & egg tarts, heat 1 tablespoon butter in a skillet, add 5 cups spinach, and cook until just wilted. Mix with 2 tablespoons heavy cream, a little grated nutmeg, salt, and pepper. Spoon into the hot tart shells, make a dip in the center, break an egg into each, then bake as above and sprinkle with shredded cheese just before serving.

spinach & pine nut tarts

Makes **6**

Preparation time **25 minutes**,
  plus chilling

Cooking time **27–28 minutes**

1 quantity **basic flaky pastry
  dough** (see page 9)
1 (8 oz) package **spinach**
2 tablespoons **butter**
1 small **onion**, finely chopped
2 **garlic cloves**, finely
  chopped
¼ teaspoon **grated nutmeg**
3 **eggs**
1 cup **crème fraîche**
3 tablespoons **pine nuts**
salt and **pepper**

Roll the pastry out thinly on a lightly floured surface
and use to line 6 buttered, 4 inch loose-bottom fluted
tart pans, rekneading and rerolling the dough trimmings
as needed. Trim off the excess dough from the top of
each tart with scissors so that it stands a little above
the pan. Put on a baking sheet and chill for 15 minutes.

Rinse the spinach well, drain in a colander, then
dry-sauté with just the water clinging to the leaves for
2–3 minutes, until the leaves have just wilted. Scoop
out of the saucepan with a slotted spoon, pressing out
any excess moisture, then finely chop the leaves.

Drain and dry the pan, then heat the butter and sauté
the onion for 5 minutes, until softened. Stir in the garlic,
cook briefly, then return the spinach to the pan. Season
with nutmeg and salt and pepper.

Beat the eggs in a bowl, add the crème fraîche, and
mix until smooth, then mix with the spinach. Divide
among the tarts and sprinkle with the pine nuts.

Bake in a preheated oven, at 350°F, for 20 minutes,
until the filling is set and the pine nuts are golden.
Check after 15 minutes and cover the tops of the tarts
loosely with aluminum foil if they seem to be browning
too quickly. Let cool for 5 minutes, then remove from
the pans and serve with a green salad.

For spinach & Stilton tarts, make the tart shells
and filling as above, but mix the eggs with 1 cup
milk and 5 oz Stilton, crumbled, instead of the crème
fraîche and nutmeg, and bake the tarts without the
pine nut topping.

pumpkin & tomato pies

Makes **4**
Preparation time **30 minutes**
Cooking time **40–45 minutes**

1 tablespoon **olive oil**
1 large **red onion**, chopped
3 cups seeded, peeled,
    and diced **pumpkin** or
    butternut squash
2 cloves **garlic**, finely chopped
½ teaspoon **smoked paprika**
1⅔ cups canned **diced
    tomatoes**
1 quantity **basic flaky pastry
    dough** (see page 9)
⅔ cup drained, crumbled **feta
    cheese**
beaten egg, to glaze
salt and **pepper**

Heat the oil in a saucepan, add the onion and pumpkin, and sauté for 5 minutes, until softened. Stir in the garlic and paprika, then the tomatoes and a little salt and pepper. Cover and simmer for 15 minutes, stirring from time to time, until the pumpkin is just cooked.

Cut the dough into 4 pieces, then roll each piece out on a lightly floured surface until large enough to line a buttered, 5 inch loose-bottomed fluted tart pan. Press over the bottom and sides, then trim the top level with the pan. Reserve the dough trimmings.

Put the pans on a baking sheet, spoon in the pumpkin filling, then sprinkle with crumbled feta. Brush the top edge of the pastry with a little beaten egg. Roll out the dough trimmings and cut into narrow strips, long enough to go over the tops of the pies. Arrange as a lattice on each pie, then brush with a little egg.

Bake the pies in a preheated oven, at 350°F, for 20–25 minutes, until golden brown. Let stand for 5 minutes, then remove from the pans and serve warm or cold.

For pumpkin & bacon pies, make up the filling and pastry shells as above, omitting the feta, and adding 4 broiled bacon slices, diced and mixed into the filling. Add the pastry lattice and bake as above.

pizza puff pies

Makes **6**
Preparation time **25 minutes**
Cooking time **40 minutes**

1 tablespoon **olive oil**
1 **onion**, chopped
1 **garlic clove**, finely chopped
1⅔ cups canned **diced
  tomatoes**
1 teaspoon **superfine sugar**
16 oz **store-bought puff
  pastry**, defrosted if frozen
small bunch of **basil**
4 oz **mozzarella cheese**,
  drained
6 **pitted ripe black olives**
  (optional)
salt and **pepper**
olive oil, to serve (optional)

Heat the oil in a saucepan, add the onion, and sauté
for 5 minutes, until softened. Add the garlic, tomatoes,
and sugar, and season with salt and pepper. Cover and
simmer gently for 15 minutes, stirring from time to
time, until the sauce has thickened. Let cool slightly.

Cut the pastry into 6, then roll out each piece on a
lightly floured surface and trim to a 6 inch circle using
a saucer as a guide. Press each pastry circle into the
bottom of a lightly oiled, metal tart pan, 4 inches in
diameter and 1 inch deep, and press the pastry at
intervals to the sides of the pan to create a wavy edge.

Reserve half the smaller basil leaves for garnish, tear
the larger leaves into pieces, and stir into the sauce.
Divide the sauce among the pies and spread into an
even layer. Cut the mozzarella into 6 slices and add a
slice to each pie. Sprinkle the mozzarella with a little
salt and pepper, and add an olive to each, if using.

Bake in a preheated oven, at 400°F, for 20 minutes,
until the pastry is crisp and golden. Let cool for
5 minutes, then turn out. Drizzle with a little olive oil,
if desired, sprinkle with the remaining basil leaves,
and serve warm with salad.

For mushroom & anchovy puff pies, add 1¾ cups
sliced white button mushrooms to the tomato sauce
for the last 5 minutes of cooking. Spoon the sauce
into the pies, top with mozzarella, and omit the olives.
Halve 6 anchovy fillets from a 2 oz can, arrange two
halves as a cross on top of each pie, then bake and
garnish as above.

french onion tarts

Makes **12**

Preparation time **30 minutes**, plus chilling

Cooking time **30–35 minutes**

1 quantity **all-butter basic flaky pastry dough** (see page 9)

4 tablespoons **butter**

2 **onions**, thinly sliced

4 **eggs**

¾ cup plus 2 tablespoons **milk**

2 teaspoons **Dijon mustard**

1 cup finely shredded **Gruyère cheese**

salt and **pepper**

Roll the dough out thinly on a lightly floured surface, then stamp out twelve 4 inch circles with a plain cookie cutter, and press into a buttered 12-cup muffin pan. Reknead and reroll the dough trimmings as needed. Chill for 15 minutes.

Heat the butter in a skillet, add the onions, and sauté over gentle heat for 10 minutes, stirring from time to time, until softened and just beginning to color.

Add the eggs, milk, and mustard to a small bowl and beat together with a fork until just mixed. Add the cheese and seasoning and mix together. Divide the mixture among the pastry shells, then spoon in the sautéed onions.

Bake the tarts in a preheated oven, at 375°F, for 20–25 minutes, until golden brown and the filling is just set. Let cool for 10 minutes, then loosen the edges of the tarts with a knife and remove from the pans. Serve warm or cold with salad.

For onion & chorizo tarts, heat 2 tablespoons butter in a skillet, add 1 sliced onion, and 4 oz diced chorizo sausage, and sauté until the onions are softened and just beginning to brown. Using a fork, mix together 4 eggs, ¾ cup plus 2 tablespoons milk, 1 cup shredded Gruyère, a few fresh thyme leaves, and salt and pepper. Add the custard to the pastry shells, then the onion and chorizo mix, and cook as above.

salmon & zucchini tarts

Makes **4**

Preparation time **30 minutes**, plus chilling

Cooking time **30–40 minutes**

1 quantity **all-butter basic flaky pastry dough** (see page 9)

2 **salmon steaks**, about 5 oz each

2 tablespoons **butter**

4 **scallions**, thinly sliced

1 small **zucchini**, diced

2 **eggs**

⅔ cup **milk**

2 teaspoons finely chopped **tarragon**

½ cup shredded **cheddar cheese**

salt and **pepper**

Divide the dough into 4 pieces, then roll each piece out on a lightly floured surface until large enough to line the bottom and sides of a buttered, 5 inch loose-bottomed fluted tart pan. Lift the dough into the pans, press over the bottom and sides, then trim the top of the dough with scissors so it stands a little above the top of the pans. Put on a baking sheet and chill for 15 minutes while making the filling.

Put the salmon in the top of a steamer, cover, and cook for 8–10 minutes, until the salmon can be broken into flakes easily and the flakes are pale pink all the way through. Lift out and put onto a plate, remove the skin (if there is any), and break into flakes, checking for and removing any bones.

Heat the butter in a small skillet, add the scallions and zucchini, and sauté gently for 3–4 minutes, until softened. Beat together the eggs, milk, and tarragon with a little salt and pepper, then stir in the cheese.

Pour the egg mixture into the tarts, add the flaked fish and the zucchini mixture, and bake in a preheated oven, at 375°F, for 20–25 minutes, until golden and the filling is just set. Serve warm or cold.

For creamy shrimp & crab tarts, sauté 1 small onion in 2 tablespoons butter until softened. Add 2 seeded and diced tomatoes and cook for 2 minutes. Beat 2 eggs with ⅔ cup mixed heavy cream and milk, ½ cup shredded cheddar, salt, cayenne pepper, and 1 (1½ oz) can dark crab meat. Pour into the tart shells, then add 5 oz cooked, peeled shrimp, defrosted if frozen. Bake as above.

creamy mushroom & stilton pies

Makes **8**

Preparation time **30 minutes**, plus cooling

Cooking time **25 minutes**

2 tablespoons **butter**

1 tablespoon **olive oil**

1 **onion**, finely chopped

8 oz mixed **mushrooms**, sliced

2 **garlic cloves**, finely chopped

3 sprigs **thyme**, leaves torn from stems

16 oz **store-bought puff pastry**, defrosted if frozen

½ cup **crème fraîche**

6 oz **Stilton cheese**, rind removed and diced

beaten egg, to glaze

salt and **pepper**

Heat the butter and oil in a skillet, add the onion, and sauté for a few minutes until just beginning to soften, then add the mushrooms and garlic and sauté, stirring until golden. Remove from the heat, add the thyme leaves, and let cool.

Roll the pastry out thinly on a lightly floured surface and trim to a 14 inch square, then cut into 16 squares. Spoon the mushroom mixture over the center of 8 of the squares, then top with crème fraîche and cheese. Brush the edges of the pastry with egg, then cover each with a second pastry square.

Press the edges of the pastry together well and crimp the edges, if desired. Transfer to a baking sheet, then slash the tops with a knife, brush with beaten egg, and sprinkle with salt flakes and extra thyme, if desired. Bake in a preheated oven, at 400°F, for 20 minutes until well risen and golden brown. Serve warm with a salad.

For deviled mushroom pies, add 8 oz sliced cup mushrooms to the fried onion as above, sauté until golden, then add 1 teaspoon Worcestershire sauce, 1 teaspoon English mustard, 1 teaspoon tomato paste, and 2 chopped tomatoes. Sauté for a few minutes until the tomatoes are softened, then cool and add to the pastry squares as above.

caribbean chicken patties

Makes **4**

Preparation time **30 minutes**, plus chilling

Cooking time **30–35 minutes**

2 tablespoons **sunflower oil**

8 oz boneless, skinless **chicken breast**, diced

2 cups seeded, peeled, and diced **butternut squash** small dice

1 small **onion**, chopped

2 **garlic cloves**, finely chopped

½ small **hot bonnet chile**, seeded and finely chopped

1 **red** or **orange bell pepper**, seeded and diced

1 teaspoon **mild curry powder** or **paste**

2 tablespoons chopped **cilantro**

beaten egg, to glaze

pepper

For the pastry dough

2 cups **all-purpose flour**

1½ teaspoons **turmeric**

½ cup diced **shortening**

2½–3 tablespoons **cold water**

salt

Make the dough. Add flour, turmeric, a little salt, and the shortening to a mixing bowl, and rub with your fingertips or using an electric mixer until you have fine crumbs. Gradually mix in enough of the measured water to form a soft but not sticky dough. Knead lightly, then wrap in plastic wrap and chill while making the filling.

Heat the oil in a skillet, add the chicken and butternut squash, and sauté for 5 minutes, until the chicken is just beginning to brown. Add the onion, garlic, chile, and bell pepper and sauté for 5 minutes, until the vegetables are softened and the chicken cooked through. Add the curry powder, cilantro, and a little pepper and cook briefly, then remove from the heat and let cool.

Cut the dough into 4 pieces, roll each piece out on a lightly floured surface, and trim to a 7 inch circle. Divide the filling among the dough circles, brush the edges with beaten egg, then fold in half and press the edges together well, first with your fingertips, then with the tines of a fork, until well sealed.

Transfer to an oiled baking sheet, brush the patties with beaten egg, and bake in a preheated oven, at 375°F, for 20–25 minutes. Serve hot or cold with chile tomato chutney.

For cheesy chile patties, omit the chicken when sautéing the butternut squash. Omit the curry powder and add ⅔ cup frozen corn kernels, defrosted, and ¾ cup diced cheddar cheese when adding the cilantro, but add to a cooled instead of hot filling.

savoyarde potato pies

Makes **4**
Preparation time **30 minutes**
Cooking time **35–45 minutes**

9–12 **new potatoes** (about
   1 lb), scrubbed and thinly
   sliced
2 tablespoons **butter**
3 **shallots**, thinly sliced, plus
   1 large **shallot**, cut into
   4 thick slices
3 **garlic cloves**, finely
   chopped
1 cup **heavy cream**
1 **egg yolk**
2 tablespoons chopped
   chives
2 teaspoons chopped **thyme**,
   plus extra leaves to decorate
¼ teaspoon **grated nutmeg**
16 oz **store-bought puff
   pastry**, defrosted if frozen
1 cup shredded **Swiss
   cheese**
beaten egg, to glaze
1 large **shallot**, cut into 4 thick
   slices
salt and **pepper**

Add the potatoes to a large saucepan of boiling water,
bring back to a boil, then cook for 3–4 minutes, until
just tender. Transfer to a colander and drain well.

Heat the butter in a skillet, add the shallots and garlic,
and sauté for 4–5 minutes, until softened and just
turning golden. Mix together the cream, egg yolk, herbs,
nutmeg, and a generous amount of salt and pepper.

Cut the pastry into 4, then roll out each piece thinly on
a lightly floured surface to a rough 8 inch circle. Use to
line 4 buttered, individual 4 inch springform pans, letting
the excess pastry hang over the sides.

Divide half the potatoes among the pans, then top with
the shallots, cheese, and the rest of the potatoes. Cover
with the cream mixture, squeeze the ends of the pastry
together to enclose the filling, trimming off any excess,
and brush the edges with beaten egg to stick together.

Brush the tops with beaten egg, add a slice of shallot
on top, and sprinkle with thyme, salt, and pepper. Bake
in a preheated oven, at 400°F, for 30–35 minutes.
Check after 20 minutes and cover with aluminum foil
if the pastry is browning too quickly.

Stand for 5 minutes, loosen the edges with a knife, remove
the pans, and serve hot with an arugula and bacon salad.

For mustard potato & pastrami pie, make the pies
as above, omitting the herbs and adding 2 teaspoons
whole-grain mustard instead. Layer the sliced
potatoes and onion with 4 oz sliced pastrami instead
of the cheese. Top with the rest of the potatoes, then
the mustard cream mixture. Continue as above.

mini raised chicken & chorizo pies

Makes **6**

Preparation time **40 minutes**, plus cooling

Cooking time **45 minutes**

10 oz good-quality **bulk sausage** or **sausage meat with the casing removed**

8 oz **skinless, boneless chicken breasts** , diced

4 oz **chorizo sausage**, diced

⅓ cup drained, chopped **sun-dried tomatoes in olive oil**

6 **scallions**, chopped

2 tablespoons chopped **rosemary**

milk, to glaze

salt and **cayenne pepper**

coarse sea salt and **paprika** to decorate (optional)

For the hot water crust pastry dough

¾ cup plus 1 tablespoon **lard**

¾ cup **milk** and **water**, mixed half and half

3 cups **all-purpose flour**

¼ teaspoon **salt**

¼ teaspoon **cayenne pepper**

Make the hot water crust pastry dough as on page 11, adding the cayenne pepper with the flour and salt. Let cool for 10–20 minutes while making the filling.

Mix together the bulk sausage, chicken, and chorizo, then add the sun-dried tomatoes, scallions, and rosemary. Season generously with salt and cayenne pepper.

Reserve one-third of the dough and cut the remainder into 6 pieces. Press one piece over the bottom and sides of an ungreased individual springform pan, 4 inches in diameter and 1¾ inches deep. Repeat with the remaining portions of dough until 6 pans have been lined.

Divide the filling among the pies and press into an even layer. Cut the reserved dough into 6 and roll out on a lightly floured surface into circles the same size as the pans. Place on top and press the edges together to seal.

Flute the edges (see page 17). Make 4 tiny steam vents in the top of the pies, then brush with milk and sprinkle with sea salt and paprika, if desired.

Bake in a preheated oven, at 350°F, for 45 minutes until golden brown and the filling is cooked. Check after 30 minutes and cover the tops loosely with aluminum foil if they seem to be browning too quickly. Cool for at least 30 minutes, then loosen the edges with a knife and remove the pans. Transfer to a wire rack and let cool completely.

For mini raised chicken & chutney pies, omit the chorizo and sun-dried tomatoes, adding 4 oz bacon, diced. Press half the filling into the pastry shells, spoon 3 tablespoons chutney among the pies, then top with the remaining filling and pastry lids as above.

stilton & leek tarts

Serves **4**
Preparation time **15 minutes**
Cooking time **25 minutes**

1 teaspoon **olive oil**
8 small **leeks**, trimmed and
  finely sliced
½ cup crumbled **Stilton**
  cheese
1 teaspoon chopped **thyme**
2 **eggs**, beaten
¼ cup **crème fraîche**
12 (6 inch) squares of **phyllo**
  pastry
milk, for brushing

Heat the oil in a saucepan, add the leeks, and sauté for
3–4 minutes, until softened.

Stir half the Stilton and the thyme into the leek mixture,
then blend together the remaining Stilton, the eggs, and
crème fraîche in a bowl.

Brush the phyllo squares with a little milk and use
them to line 4 fluted pans, each 4 inches in diameter.
Spoon the leek mixture into the pans, then pour over
the cheese and egg mixture.

Put the pans on a baking sheet and bake in a
preheated oven, at 400°F, for 15–20 minutes,
until the filling is set, then serve.

For scallion & cheddar tarts, use the same quantity
of sharp cheddar cheese instead of Stilton and shred
it coarsely. Slice 2 bunches of large scallions instead
of the leeks and sauté for 1 minute, then remove from
the heat. Add the scallions to the cheese mixture and
continue as above.

turkey & cranberry turnovers

Makes **6**
Preparation time **25 minutes**
Cooking time **20 minutes**

1 tablespoon **sunflower oil**
1 **onion**, chopped
8 oz **ground turkey**
4 **smoked bacon slices**,
  diced
½ teaspoon **dried mixed
  herbs**
16 oz **store-bought puff
  pastry**, defrosted if frozen
3 tablespoons **cranberry
  sauce**
beaten egg, to glaze
salt and **pepper**

Heat the oil in a skillet, add the onion, turkey, and bacon, and sauté, stirring, for 5 minutes, until golden. Remove from the heat and stir in the dried herbs and salt and pepper. Let cool.

Roll the pastry out thinly on a lightly floured surface and trim to a 10 × 20 inch rectangle, then cut into eight 5 inch squares. Divide the turkey mixture among the squares, top each with a little cranberry sauce, then brush the edges of the pastry with beaten egg.

Fold each pastry square in half to make a triangle, press the edges together well, then slash the tops with crisscross lines. Transfer to a baking sheet, then brush with beaten egg and bake in a preheated oven, at 400°F, for 15–20 minutes, until well risen and golden. Serve hot or cold.

For chicken & chutney turnovers, add 8 oz skinless, boneless chicken breasts, diced to the sautéed onion and bacon, cook until golden, then mix with the dried herbs and seasoning. Add to the pastry squares and top with 3 tablespoons tomato chutney.

main meals

mediterranean vegetable pie

Serves **4**
Preparation time **30 minutes**
Cooking time **60–65 minutes**

2 large **eggplants**, sliced
⅓ cup **olive oil**
1 large **red onion**, chopped
3 **garlic cloves**, finely chopped
1⅔ cups canned **diced
tomatoes**
½ cup **red wine**
1 teaspoon **superfine sugar**
4 teaspoons finely chopped
rosemary
2 **roasted red peppers** from a
jar, drained and quartered
beaten egg, to glaze
salt and **pepper**

For Parmesan pastry dough
3 cups **all-purpose flour**
6 tablespoons **butter** and
⅓ cup plus 1 tablespoon
shortening, diced
½ cup grated **Parmesan
cheese**, plus extra for
sprinkling
2 tablespoons finely chopped
rosemary, plus extra for
sprinkling
4–4½ tablespoons **cold water**
salt

Arrange the eggplant slices on a foil-lined broiler rack,
drizzle with 2 tablespoons oil, and sprinkle with salt and
pepper. Broil for 5 minutes, until browned, then oil and
season the other side and broil for 5 minutes; set aside.

Heat the remaining oil in a saucepan, add the onion,
and sauté for 5 minutes, until softened. Add the garlic,
tomatoes, wine, sugar, and rosemary, and season with
salt and pepper. Simmer, uncovered, for 15 minutes,
stirring occasionally, until thickened, then let cool.

Make the dough. Add the flour and a pinch of salt to a
bowl, then rub in the fats with your fingertips or an electric
mixer until you have fine crumbs. Stir in the Parmesan
and rosemary, then mix in enough of the water to form a
soft but not sticky dough. Knead lightly, then cut in half.

Roll one dough half out thinly on a lightly floured board
Ito cover a buttered 10 inch metal pie plate. Lift the dough
into the pie plate, then spoon one-third of the tomato
sauce over the bottom. Arrange half the eggplants on top,
cover with half the remaining sauce, then the roasted
peppers. Repeat with the remaining eggplants and sauce.

Roll out the remaining dough to form a lid. Brush the
edge of the dough on the plate with beaten egg. Lift
the lid over the pie, press the edges together, and trim.
Brush the top of the pie with egg, and sprinkle with
rosemary and a little Parmesan. Bake in a preheated
oven, at 375°F, for 30–35 minutes, until golden. Check
after 20 minutes and cover with aluminum foil if needed.

For lamb & eggplant pie, cook only 1 sliced eggplant
with 1 tablespoon olive oil and add 8 oz ground lamb
when sautéing the onion.

picnic pie

Serves **6–8**
Preparation time **35 minutes**
Cooking time **1½ hours**

1 lb **pork sausages**, skinned
1 lb boneless, skinless
  chicken thighs, chopped
4 oz **smoked bacon**, diced
5 **cloves**, coarsely crushed
¼ teaspoon **ground allspice**
small bunch of **sage**
1 **Braeburn apple**, cored and
  sliced
1 **egg yolk** mixed with
  1 tablespoon **water**
salt and **pepper**

**For the hot water crust pastry
dough**
¾ cup plus 1 tablespoon **lard**
⅓ cup **milk** mixed with ⅓ cup
  water
2 teaspoons **English mustard**
3 cups **all-purpose flour**
¼ teaspoon **salt**

Make the hot water crust pastry dough according to the method on page 11, stirring the mustard into the melted lard mixture. Cool for 10 minutes.

Mix together the sausage, chicken, bacon, cloves, allspice, and plenty of salt and pepper in a bowl.

Reserve one-third of the dough, press the remaining warm dough over the bottom and sides of a deep 7 inch loose-bottom cake pan. Spoon in half the meat filling and level. Cover with half the sage leaves, then the apple slices, and spoon the rest of the filling over the top. Level and top with the remaining sage. Brush the edges of the dough with the egg glaze.

Roll out the reserved dough to a circle a little larger than the pan, arrange on the pie and press the edges together. Trim off the excess, then crimp the edge. Roll out the trimmings and decorate (see page 17). Make a slit in the top of the pie, then brush with the egg glaze. Cook in a preheated oven, at 350°F, for 1½ hours, covering with aluminum foil after 40 minutes, when golden. Let cool, then remove the pan. Put the pie, still on the loose pan bottom, in the refrigerator for 3–4 hours or overnight. When ready to serve, remove the bottom and cut the pie into wedges.

For apricot & pickled onion pie, make the filling as above, but omit the sage and apples and replace with ¾ cup sliced dried apricots and 3½ oz pickled onions, drained and sliced.

salmon & asparagus en croûte

Serves **4**
Preparation time **25 minutes**
Cooking time **40–45 minutes**

2 tablespoons **butter**
6 oz **asparagus**, trimmed
1 lb–1¼ lb **salmon fillet**,
   about 7–8 inches long,
   skinned
juice of ½ **lemon**
16 oz **store-bought puff
   pastry**, defrosted if frozen
½ cup **reduced-fat cream
   cheese**
grated rind of **1 lemon**
1 tablespoon chopped
   tarragon
2 tablespoons chopped
   parsley
1½ teaspoons **green
   peppercorns**, drained and
   chopped (optional)
⅓ cup drained, coarsely
   chopped **sundried
   tomatoes in oil**
beaten egg, to glaze
salt flakes, for sprinkling
salt and **pepper**

Heat the butter in a skillet, add the asparagus, and sauté for 2–3 minutes, until just softened, then season with salt and pepper. Drizzle the salmon with lemon juice and season.

Roll the pastry out thinly on a lightly floured surface and trim to a 14 inch square, then trim a 1½ inch strip off one of the sides. Put the salmon on top so that the long side of the salmon is parallel with the narrower side of the pastry rectangle.

Dot the cheese on top of the salmon, then sprinkle with the lemon rind, herbs, peppercorns, if using, and tomatoes. Arrange the asparagus on top, alternating their direction.

Brush the pastry around the salmon with beaten egg, then fold the narrower sides up and over the salmon, pressing to seal. Cut the excess from the top ends of pastry, then fold and press to wrap the fish like a package.

Brush the package with beaten egg and transfer to a baking sheet. Decorate (see page 17), and sprinkle with salt flakes, if liked. Bake in a preheated oven, at 400°F, for 35–40 minutes. Check after 25 minutes and cover with aluminum foil if the pastry seems to be browning too quickly. To test if the salmon is cooked, insert a knife into the center, wait 3 seconds, then remove; if the knife feels hot, it is cooked. Cut into thick slices and serve with lemon wedges.

For salmon & watercress en croûte, add 1 torn bunch of watercress to a food processor with the cheese, grated lemon rind, and a little salt and pepper, and blend until smooth. Spread over the salmon fillet on the pastry, then wrap the pastry around as above.

chicken & mushroom pies

Makes **4**

Preparation time **35 minutes**,
    plus chilling

Cooking time **1 hour
    10 minutes**

1 tablespoon **olive oil**

8 boneless, skinless **chicken
    thighs**, about 1¼ lb, cubed

1 **onion**, chopped

2 **garlic cloves**, finely chopped

2 tablespoons **all-purpose
    flour**

⅔ cup **white wine**

1 cup **chicken stock**

few sprigs **thyme** or a little
    dried thyme

2 tablespoons **butter**

1⅔ cups sliced **mushrooms**

beaten egg, to glaze

salt and **pepper**

For the pastry dough

2⅓ cups plus 1 tablespoon
    all-purpose flour

1½ teaspoons **mustard
    powder**

6 tablespoons **butter** and
    ⅓ cup plus 1 tablespoon
    shortening, diced

3 tablespoons **cold water**

salt and **pepper**

Heat the oil in a large skillet and cook the chicken, stirring, until beginning to color. Add the onion and cook until the chicken is golden and the onion softened. Stir in the garlic, then mix in the flour. Add the wine, stock, thyme, and a sprinkle of salt and pepper. Bring to the boil, stirring, then cover and simmer for 30 minutes.

Heat the butter in a small skillet, add the mushrooms, and sauté until golden. Add to the chicken and let cool.

Make the pastry dough. Add the flour, mustard, and a little salt and pepper to a mixing bowl. Add the fats and rub in using your fingertips or using an electric mixer until you have fine crumbs. Gradually mix in enough of the water to form a soft but not sticky dough. Knead lightly, wrap in pastic wrap, and chill for 15 minutes.

Reserve one-third of the dough, and cut the rest into 4 pieces. Roll each piece out thinly, then line 4 buttered, individual springform pans, 4 inches in diameter and 1¾ inches deep. Roll out the reserved dough thinly and cut out lids, using the pans as a guide.

Spoon the chicken filling into the pies, brush the top edges with beaten egg, then add the lids and press the pastry edges together. Flute the edges and bake on a baking sheet in a preheated oven, at 375°C, for 30 minutes, until golden. Let stand for 5 minutes, then loosen the edges, transfer to a plate, and remove the pans. Serve with green vegetables.

For chicken & bacon pies, reduce the amount of chicken to 1 lb and add 4 oz diced bacon when sautéing the chicken and onion.

summer shrimp & fish phyllo pie

Serves **4**
Preparation time **10 minutes**
Cooking time **20–25 minutes**

1 ½ lb **skinless white fish
  fillets**
4 oz **frozen cooked, peeled
  shrimp**, defrosted
⅔ cup **frozen peas**, defrosted
grated rind and juice of
  1 lemon
2 ½ cups **store-bought
  white sauce**
1 bunch of **dill**, chopped
8 sheets of **phyllo pastry**
melted butter, for brushing
salt and **pepper**

Cut the fish into large, bite-size pieces and put in a
bowl with the shrimp and peas. Add the lemon rind and
juice, stir in the white sauce and dill, and season well
with salt and pepper.

Transfer the fish mixture to a casserole or pie dish.
Cover the surface with the sheets of phyllo pastry,
scrunching up each sheet into a loosely crumpled ball.
Brush the pastry with melted butter.

Bake the pie in a preheated oven, at 400°F, for
20–25 minutes, until the pastry is golden brown and
the fish is cooked through.

For seafood & potato pie, prepare the fish mixture
as above, but use 2 tablespoons chopped parsley
in place of the dill. Put into a medium ovenproof
dish. Cook 6 medium potatoes (about 1 lb 10 oz),
chopped, in a large saucepan of salted boiling water
until tender. Meanwhile, put 2 extra-large eggs in
a separate saucepan and bring to a boil. Cook for
10 minutes, then plunge into cold water to cool.
Shell the eggs and cut in half lengthwise. Drain the
potatoes and mash with 2 tablespoons butter. Season
well with salt and pepper. Gently press the egg
halves, at evenly spaced intervals, into the fish mixture,
then spoon or pipe the mashed potato over the fish
mixture. Bake as above until the top is lightly golden
and the fish is cooked through.

chili beef packages

Makes **6**
Preparation time **30 minutes**
Cooking time **1 hour 10 minutes**

2 teaspoons **sunflower oil**
8 oz **minced beef**
1 small **onion**, chopped
1 **garlic clove**, finely chopped
½ teaspoon **crushed red pepper**
¼ teaspoon **ground cinnamon**
2 teaspoons **light brown sugar**
1 **bay leaf**
⅔ cup canned **diced tomatoes**
½ (15 oz) can **red kidney beans**, drained
⅔ cup **beef stock**
beaten egg, to glaze
salt and **pepper**

For cornmeal pastry dough
2⅓ cups plus 1 tablespoon **all-purpose flour**
⅓ cup **cornmeal**
6 tablespoons **butter**, diced
⅓ cup plus 1 tablespoon **shortening**, diced
4–4½ tablespoons **cold water**

Heat the oil in a saucepan, add the beef and onion, and sauté, stirring, until the beef is browned. Stir in the garlic, red pepper, cinnamon, sugar, and bay leaf. Mix in the tomatoes, kidney beans, and stock, then add plenty of salt and pepper. Bring to a boil, stirring, then cover and simmer gently for 45 minutes. Let cool.

Make the dough. Add the flour, cornmeal, fats, and a little salt and pepper to a bowl. Rub in the fats with your fingertips or an electric mixer until you have fine crumbs. Add enough water to form a smooth dough, then knead lightly on a surface dusted with flour.

Cut the dough in half, roll out one half and trim to a 5 × 15 inch rectangle, then cut into thee 5 inch squares. Spoon half the filling into the center of the pastry squares. Brush the edges with beaten egg, then bring the points of the pastry up to the center, pressing the straight edges of the pastry together.

Transfer to an oiled baking sheet and repeat with the remaining dough and filling to make 6 pies. Brush the pies with beaten egg, then bake in a preheated oven, at 375°F, for 20 minutes.

Serve hot with sour cream and chunky salsa.

For herbed beef pies, sauté the beef and onion as above, then stir in 1 small diced carrot, 1 teaspoon dried mixed herbs, 1 teaspoon English mustard, 1 tablespoon Worcestershire sauce, ⅔ cup canned diced tomatoes, and ⅔ cup beef stock. Cover and simmer for 45 minutes, then continue as above with a basic flaky pastry dough (see page 9).

golden mushroom & leek pies

Serves **4**
Preparation time **15 minutes**
Cooking time **25–30 minutes**

2 tablespoons **butter**
2 **leeks**, thinly sliced
10 oz **cremini mushrooms**
4 cups quartered **white button mushrooms**
1 tablespoon **all-purpose flour**
1 cup **milk**
2/3 cup **heavy cream**
1 shredded **sharp cheddar cheese**
1/4 cup finely chopped **parsley**
2 sheets of **store-bought puff pastry**, defrosted if frozen
beaten egg, to glaze

Melt the butter in a large saucepan, add the leeks, and cook for 1–2 minutes. Add the mushrooms and cook for 2 minutes. Stir in the flour and cook, stirring, for 1 minute, then gradually add the milk and cream and cook, stirring continuously, until the mixture thickens. Add the cheddar and the parsley and cook, stirring, for 1–2 minutes. Remove from the heat.

Cut 4 circles from the pastry sheets to cover 4 individual pie plates. Divide the mushroom mixture among the pie plates. Brush the rims with the beaten egg, then place the pastry circles on top. Press down around the rims and crimp the edges with a fork. Cut a couple of slits in the top of each pie to let the steam out. Brush the pastry with the remaining egg.

Bake the pies in a preheated oven, at 425°F, for 15–20 minutes, until the pastry is golden brown. Serve immediately.

For curried ham & mushroom pies, follow the first stage above, but after cooking the mushrooms, add 1 teaspoon medium curry powder and ½ teaspoon turmeric to the saucepan and cook, stirring, for 1 minute, before adding the flour and continuing with the recipe. Once the sauce has thickened, stir in 8 oz cooked ham, cut into small bite-size pieces, in place of the cheddar and ¼ cup chopped cilantro instead of the parsley. Make and bake the pies as above.

torta pasqualina

Serves **6**

Preparation time **30 minutes**,
  plus chilling

Cooking time **45–50 minutes**

1 quantity **basic flaky pastry
  dough** (see page 9)

1 (6 oz) jar **chilled
  charbrolled artichokes
  in olive oil**

1 **onion**, chopped

2 cloves **garlic**, finely chopped

1 (8 oz) package **spinach**,
  rinsed and drained

1¼ cups halved **cherry
  tomatoes**

¾ cup grated **Parmesan
  cheese**

4 **eggs**

1 cup **milk**

salt and **pepper**

Roll the dough out thinly on a lightly floured surface until a little larger than a buttered 11 × 8 inch loose-bottom, fluted rectangular tart pan. Lift the dough over a rolling pin, drape into the pan, then press over the bottom and sides. Trim off the excess dough with scissors so that it stands a little above the top of the pan. Chill for 15 minutes.

Drain off 1 tablespoon oil from the artichokes into a skillet, add the onion and garlic, and sauté for 5 minutes, until softened. Scoop out of the skillet and reserve. Add the spinach to the skillet and sauté for 2–3 minutes, until just wilted. Transfer to a strainer and press out the liquid.

Put the tart shell on a baking sheet. Arrange the spinach in the bottom of the pastry shell, drain and arrange the artichoke hearts and halved tomatoes on top, then sprinkle with the Parmesan. Beat the eggs and milk with salt and pepper and pour into the tart.

Bake the tart in a preheated oven, at 375°F, for 30–40 minutes, until golden brown and the filling is just set. Let cool for 15 minutes, then remove the tart from the pan. Cut into squares and serve warm or cold.

For Italian goat cheese tart, omit the artichokes and add 14 oz goat cheese, diced, instead.

chicken bisteeya

Serves **6**

Preparation time **40 minutes**

Cooking time **1 hour 50 minutes**

4 **chicken thighs and drumsticks**

1 **onion**, chopped

1 **cinnamon stick**, halved

1 inch piece **fresh ginger root**, finely chopped

¼ teaspoon **turmeric**

2½ cups **water**

3 tablespoons chopped **cilantro**

3 tablespoons chopped **parsley**

⅓ cup **raisins**

¼ cup **blanched almonds**, coarsely chopped

4 **eggs**

7 oz chilled **phyllo pastry**

5 tablespoons **butter**, melted

salt and **pepper**

To garnish

confectioners' sugar, sifted

ground cinnamon

Pack the chicken into a large saucepan and sprinkle the onion over the top, then add the cinnamon, ginger, turmeric, and salt and pepper. Cover the chicken with the measured water. Cover and simmer for 1 hour, until tender. Lift the chicken out of the stock and transfer to a plate to cool. Boil the stock rapidly for about 10 minutes, until reduced by one-third.

Dice the chicken, discarding the skin and bones. Strain the stock into a pitcher. Discard the cinnamon stick, then add the herbs, raisins, and almonds to the chicken. Gradually whisk ¾ cup plus 2 tablespoons of the stock into the eggs.

Brush a 9 inch springform pan with a little of the melted butter. Unfold the pastry, then place one of the sheets in the pan so that it half covers the bottom and drapes up over the side and hangs over the top of the pan. Add a second pastry sheet overlapping a little over the first and brush with a little melted butter. Continue adding pastry, brushing alternate sheets with melted butter until two-thirds of the pastry has been used and the pan is thickly covered.

Spoon in the chicken mixture, then cover with the eggs and stock. Arrange the remaining pastry over the top in a smooth layer, then fold in the sides in soft pleats, brushing layers of pastry with butter as you work. Brush the top layer with the remaining butter, then bake in a preheated oven, at 350°F, for 40–45 minutes, until golden brown and the filling is set.

Let cool for 15 minutes, then remove from the pan. Dust with the sifted sugar and cinnamon and serve warm.

game pie

Serves **4**
Preparation time **45 minutes**
Cooking time **2 hours**

2 tablespoons **butter**
1 tablespoon **olive oil**
1 **oven-ready pheasant**,
  halved
1 **oven-ready pigeon**, halved
2 **rabbit** or **chicken leg joints**
1 large **onion**, coarsely
  chopped
4 oz **smoked bacon**, diced
2 tablespoons **all-purpose**
  flour
¾ cup plus 2 tablespoons
  red wine
1¾ cups **chicken stock**
2 tablespoons **red currant**
  jelly
1 teaspoon **juniper** or **allspice**
  berries, coarsely crushed
1 **bouquet garni** (such as a
  few sprigs of parsley, bay
  leaves, and thyme tied
  together)
12 oz **store-bought puff**
  pastry, defrosted if frozen
beaten egg, to glaze
salt and **pepper**

Heat the butter and oil in a large skillet, then sauté the game, in batches, until browned. Lift out and put into a large casserole dish. Add the onion and bacon to the skillet and sauté for 5 minutes, stirring until golden. Mix in the flour, then stir in the wine, stock, and red currant jelly. Add the berries, bouquet garni, and seasoning, then bring to a boil. Pour the sauce over the game, cover, and cook in a preheated oven, at 325°F, for 1¼ hours. Let cool.

Lift out the game and take the meat off the bone. Return the meat to the sauce, discard the bouquet garni, then spoon into a 1¼ quart pie plate.

Roll out the pastry on a lightly floured surface until a little larger than the top of the pie plate. Cut ½ inch wide strips from the edges and stick onto the dish rim with beaten egg. Brush the pastry strips with egg and lay the sheet of pastry on top. Press down, trim off the excess, then flute the edges. Cut leaves from the rerolled trimmings and decorate (see page 17).

Brush the pie with beaten egg, then cook in a preheated oven, at 400°F, for 30–35 minutes, until golden and piping hot inside. Serve with steamed braised red cabbage, if liked.

For beef & mushroom pie, sauté 1½ lb diced chuck short ribs or boneless beef chuck and 2 cups quartered mushrooms in the butter and oil. Mix with the sautéed onion and bacon, then the flour and stock. Continue as above but cook for 2 hours in the oven before making the pie as above.

creamy asparagus puff pie

Serves **6**
Preparation time **25 minutes**
Cooking time **30–40 minutes**

16 oz **store-bought puff
pastry**, defrosted if frozen
1 **egg**, beaten
8 oz bunch of **asparagus**
1 bunch of **scallions**
1 tablespoon **olive oil**
½ cup **mascarpone cheese**
1 large **garlic clove**, finely
chopped
¼ cup grated **Parmesan
cheese**, plus extra for
sprinkling
salt and **pepper**

Roll out the pastry thickly on a lightly floured surface
and trim to a 9 × 12 inch rectangle. Transfer to an
oiled baking sheet and use a little beaten egg to glaze.
Mark a line 1 inch)in from the edge, then prick the
inside rectangle with a fork.

Bake in a preheated oven, at 400°F, for 10 minutes.
Press down the center with the back of a fork, then
bake for another 5–10 minutes, until the pastry is
cooked through. Press down the center once again.

Meanwhile, trim 1 inch from the bottom of the
asparagus, then trim the scallions to the same length.
Toss the asparagus and scallions in the oil and plenty
of salt and pepper, then cook in a preheated, ridged
grill pan for 5 minutes, turning, until just cooked.

Beat the mascarpone with the garlic, Parmesan,
remaining beaten egg, and salt and pepper. Spoon into
the center of the pastry shell and spread into an even
layer. Arrange the asparagus and scallions alternately
on top and sprinkle with a little extra Parmesan.

Bake for 10–15 minutes, until the filling is just set,
Check after 10 minutes and cover with aluminum foil if
the pastry seems to be browning too quickly.

For asparagus & tomato puff pie, sauté 1 chopped
onion in 1 tablespoon oil until soft, add 2 chopped garlic
cloves, 1⅔ cups canned diced tomatoes, 1 tablespoon
tomato paste, 1 teaspoon superfine sugar, salt, and
pepper. Simmer for 10 minutes, stirring, until thick.
Make the pie as above, stir the Parmesan into the
sauce, spread in the bottom of the pie, top with grilled
asparagus and scallions, then bake as above.

asian mushroom packages

Makes **4**
Preparation time **25 minutes**
Cooking time **25 minutes**

4 large **portobello mushrooms**, wiped
1 tablespoon **sesame oil**
1 tablespoon **ketjap manis** or **soy sauce**
1 inch piece **fresh ginger root**, peeled and finely chopped
2 **garlic cloves**, finely chopped
¼ cup coarsely chopped **cilantro**
1 **tomato**, cut into 4 thick slices
2 tablespoons **butter**, cut into 4 pieces
1 quantity **basic flaky pastry dough** (see page 9)
beaten egg, to glaze
4 teaspoons **sesame seeds**, for sprinkling
pepper

Trim the top of the mushroom stems level with the caps, drizzle the gills with the sesame oil and ketjap manis or soy sauce, then sprinkle with the ginger, garlic, and cilantro. Top each with a slice of tomato, a pat of butter, and a little pepper.

Divide the dough into 4 pieces, roll out one piece thinly on a lightly floured surface to a roughly shaped 7–8 inch circle, or large enough to enclose the mushrooms (this will depend on how big they are, so make a little bigger, if needed).

Place a mushroom on top of a dough circle, brush the edges with beaten egg, then lift the dough up and over the top of the mushroom, pleating the dough as you work and pinching the ends together in the center of the mushroom to completely enclose it. Repeat to make 4 packages and put them onto a buttered baking sheet.

Brush the packages with beaten egg and sprinkle with sesame seeds. Bake in a preheated oven, at 400°F, for about 25 minutes, until golden brown. Transfer to serving plates and accompany with stir-fried vegetables and soy sauce.

For French mushroom packages, drizzle 4 large portobello mushrooms with 1 tablespoon olive oil and 2 tablespoons red wine, then top with 2 finely chopped garlic cloves, 2 tablespoons chopped basil, 2 tablespoons chopped chives, and 4 slices of goat cheese cut from a 4 oz piece. Season the cheese with salt and pepper, then wrap in dough, glaze with egg, and top with a slice of onion. Bake as above.

goat cheese & beet tart

Serves **6**

Preparation time **30 minutes**,
plus chilling

Cooking time **45–50 minutes**

1 quantity **basic flaky pastry
dough** (see page 9)

1 tablespoon **olive oil**

1 **onion**, chopped

4 raw, trimmed **beets**,
coarsely shredded

4 **eggs**

1 cup **milk**

1 teaspoon **Dijon mustard**

small bunch of **thyme**

1 (5 oz) **goat cheese log**

salt and **cayenne pepper**

Roll the dough out on a lightly floured surface until a
little larger than a buttered 9½ inch loose-bottom
fluted tart pan. Lift the dough over a rolling pin, drape
into the pan, then press over the bottom and sides. Trim
off the excess dough with scissors so that it stands a
little above the top of the pan. Chill for 15 minutes.

Meanwhile, heat the oil in a skillet, add the onion,
and sauté until softened. Add the beets and cook for
2–3 minutes. Beat together the eggs, milk, and
mustard in a bowl. Add the onions, some of the thyme
leaves torn from the stems, and a generous amount of
salt and cayenne pepper. Let stand for 5 minutes.

Put the tart shell on a baking sheet and pour the beet
mixture into the tart shell. Cut the cheese into 6 thick
slices, arrange in a ring on top of the tart, and sprinkle
with the remaining thyme leaves and a little salt and
cayenne pepper.

Bake the tart in a preheated oven, at 350°F, for
40–45 minutes until the filling is set. Let cool for
15 minutes, then remove the pan and transfer to a
plate. Serve warm or cold, cut into wedges, with salad.

For minted zucchini & goat cheese tart, dice
1 medium zucchini and add to the sautéed onions,
sauté for a few additional minutes, then mix with
2 tablespoons chopped mint and 2 tablespoons
chopped chives. Beat together the eggs, milk,
mustard, and seasoning as above, then add the
zucchini mixture. Transfer to the uncooked tart shell,
arrange the goat cheese on top, season the cheese,
and bake as above.

venison & red wine pie

Serves **4**

Preparation time **25 minutes**

Cooking time **2 hours
50 minutes**

1 tablespoon **olive oil**

1 ¼ lb shoulder or leg of
  venison, diced

1 **onion**, chopped

4 **bacon slices**, diced

2 **garlic cloves**, finely
  chopped

2 tablespoons **all-purpose
  flour**

1 ¼ cups **red wine**

2 cups **beef stock**

1 tablespoon **tomato paste**

3 sprigs **rosemary**, leaves
  chopped, plus extra, torn,
  for sprinkling

2 tablespoons **butter**

10 oz **shallots**, peeled and
  halved if large

2 cups thickly sliced
  mushrooms

1 quantity **rosemary flaky
  pastry dough** (see page 10)

beaten egg, to glaze

salt and **pepper**

Heat the oil in a flameproof casserole, add the venison,
then add the onion and bacon and sauté, stirring, until
the venison is browned. Stir in the garlic and flour, then
mix in the wine, stock, and tomato paste. Add the
rosemary and season well with salt and pepper.

Bring to a boil, stirring, then cover and transfer to a
preheated oven, at 325°F, for 2 hours. Take the dish
out of the oven. Heat the butter in a skillet, add the
shallots and mushrooms, and sauté until golden, then
stir into the venison and let cool.

Spoon the venison mixture into a 1 ¼ quart pie plate.
Roll out the dough on a lightly floured surface until
about 2 inches wider than the diameter of the pie plate.
Cut 2 long strips from the edges about 1 inch wide.
Brush the plate rim with egg, press the strips on top,
then brush these with egg. Lift the pie lid in place,
sealing the edges together well. Trim the excess pastry.

Flute the edge of the dough (see page 17). Brush with
egg and sprinkle with a few extra torn rosemary leaves.
Decorate the top, if desired. Bake in a preheated oven,
at 375°F, for 35–40 minutes, until the pastry is golden
and the filling piping hot. Serve with green beans and
braised red cabbage.

For lamb & prune pie, sauté 1 ¼ lb sliced boneless
lamb in oil with the chopped onion and bacon as
above. Add the garlic, flour, red wine, and stock, then
stir in the rosemary, 1 tablespoon red currant jelly, and
10 pitted and halved prunes (dried plums). Season and
cook as above, then add the shallots and mushrooms.
Top with the dough and bake as above.

mixed seafood puff pies

Makes **4**
Preparation time **30 minutes**
Cooking time **40–45 minutes**

10 oz **white fish fillets**, such
as cod or haddock
10 oz **salmon fillet**, cut into
2 pieces
2½ cups **milk**
2 **bay leaves**
rind of **1 lemon**, pared into
strips with a vegetable
peeler
4 tablespoons **butter**
⅓ cup plus 1 tablespoon
all-purpose flour
⅔ cup **fish stock** (made with
half a bouillon cube)
¾ cup **corn kernels**
1 bunch of **scallions**, finely
sliced
1 cup shredded **cheddar
cheese**
12 oz **frozen mixed seafood**,
defrosted, rinsed with cold
water, and drained
16 oz **store-bought puff
pastry**, defrosted if frozen
beaten egg, to glaze
salt and **pepper**

Lay the fish fillets in a skillet, pour over just enough milk to cover, then add the bay leaves, lemon rind, and salt and pepper. Cover and simmer for 8 minutes or until the fish is just cooked and flakes easily.

Lift the fish out onto a plate, peel away the skin, then break into large flakes, removing any bones. Strain the milk and mix with the remaining milk.

Heat the butter in a saucepan, stir in the flour, and cook briefly, then gradually mix in the milk and bring to a boil, stirring. Stir in the fish stock and cook over low heat for 3–4 minutes. Stir in the corn, scallions, and cheese, then season generously with salt and pepper. Cover the surface of the sauce with wetted wax paper or nonstick parchment paper and let cool.

Fold the flaked fish and mixed seafood into the sauce, then spoon into 4 individual round pie plates. Roll the pastry out thinly on a lightly floured surface and cut out 4 pastry lids. Brush the plate rims with egg and press the lids in place. Cut fish shapes from the pastry trimmings and arrange on top, then glaze with egg.

Bake the pies in a preheated oven, at 400°F, for 25–30 minutes, until the pastry is well risen and golden and the filling is piping hot.

For smoked fish & egg puff pies, first poach 10 oz haddock fillets and 10 oz smoked haddock in the milk, bay leaves, and lemon rind as above. Make the sauce as above, stir in the corn, scallions, and cheese, then the flaked fish, 8 oz shrimp, defrosted if frozen, and 3 hard-boiled, shelled, and diced eggs. Add the pie lids and cook as above.

clam, leek & ham pies

Makes **6**

Preparation time **45 minutes**,
plus chilling

Cooking time **50–55 minutes**

2½ cups **milk**

2 **leeks**, trimmed, thinly sliced,
white and green parts kept
separate

2 **bay leaves**

8 oz **cured ham** or **cooked
ham steak**

4 tablespoons **butter**

⅓ cup plus 1 tablespoon
all-purpose flour

8 oz **small baby clams**,
defrosted if frozen

beaten egg, to glaze

salt and **pepper**

For the pastry dough

3 cups **all-purpose flour**

6 tablespoons **butter** and
⅓ cup plus 1 tablespoon
shortening, diced

4–4½ tablespoons **cold water**

salt and **pepper**

Pour the milk into a saucepan, add the white sliced leeks, bay leaves, and salt and pepper, then bring to the boil. Set aside for 10 minutes. Broil the ham steak on a foil-lined broiler pan for 7–8 minutes, turning once, until cooked. Trim off the fat, then dice the meat.

Heat the butter in a saucepan, stir in the flour, cook for 1–2 minutes, then gradually mix in the strained milk. Bring to a boil, stirring until smooth. Discard the bay leaves, then return the white leeks to the sauce, add the green sliced leeks, and cook gently for 2–3 minutes, stirring until the leeks are just cooked. Let cool.

Make the dough according to the method on page 9. Wrap the dough in plastic wrap and chill for 15 minutes.

Reserve one-third of the dough, roll out the remainder thinly, then cut six 6 inch circles. Press into buttered individual tart pans, 4 inches) in diameter and 1 inch deep. Trim off the excess dough and reknead and reroll the trimmings as needed.

Stir the clams and diced ham into the sauce, then spoon into the pie shells. Brush the edges with egg. Roll out the reserved dough and cut 5 inch circles for the lids. Press the dough edges together and flute (see page 17), prick the top to let steam escape, then brush with beaten egg. Decorate (see page 17) and sprinkle with salt and pepper.

Bake the pies on a baking sheet in a preheated oven, at 375°F, for 30–35 minutes, until golden brown. Serve with steamed baby carrots.

sweet pies

mixed berry mille feuilles

Makes **6**
Preparation time **30 minutes**,
plus chilling
Cooking time **15 minutes**

12 oz **store-bought puff
  pastry**, defrosted if frozen
4 cups **mixed berries**
  (about 1 lb), including sliced
  strawberries and raspberries,
  and a few blueberries
3 tablespoons **confectioners'
  sugar**

For the vanilla custard
2 **egg yolks**
¼ cup **superfine sugar**
3 tablespoons **all-purpose
  flour**
3 tablespoons **cornstarch**
⅔ cup **heavy cream**
⅔ cup **milk**
1 teaspoon **vanilla extract**

Roll the pastry out on a lightly floured surface and trim
to a 12 × 7½ inch rectangle, then cut into nine 4 ×
2½ inch rectangles. Transfer to an oiled baking sheet,
leaving space between them, then chill for 15 minutes.

Bake the pastry in a preheated oven, at 400°F, for
10–12 minutes, until well risen and golden. Transfer
to a wire rack to cool.

Make the vanilla custard filling. Beat together the egg
yolks and sugar in a large bowl, then mix in the flours.
Pour the cream and milk into a saucepan, bring to a
boil, then gradually beat into the yolks until smooth.
Pour back into the saucepan and heat, beating
continuously, until thick. Beat in the vanilla extract, then
remove from the heat, cover the surface with a piece of
crumpled and wetted parchment paper and let cool.

Split each pastry in half through the center. Sandwich
3 pastry halves together with the cooked custard and
fruit. Repeat to make 6 pastry stacks.

Sift the confectioner's sugar over the stacks. Heat
3 metal skewers in a gas flame or under the broiler until
hot. Press them into the confectioners' sugar until they
form caramelized lines in the sugar. Repeat, warming the
skewers between applications when needed.

For lemon cream mille feuilles, beat 1 cup heavy
cream until it forms soft swirls. Fold in 3 tablespoons
lemon curd and sandwich the pastries together with
the cream instead of vanilla custard. Mix ¾ cup
confectioners' sugar, sifted, with 1 tablespoon fresh
lemon juice to a smooth icing, spoon over the tops of
the pastries, and decorate with lemon rind curls.

peach melba pie

Serves **6**

Preparation time **40 minutes**,
plus cooling

Cooking time **30–35 minutes**

1 quantity **all-butter sweet
basic flaky pastry dough**
(see page 10)

⅓ cup **superfine sugar**,
plus extra for sprinkling

1 teaspoon **cornstarch**

grated rind of 1 **lemon**

5 **peaches** (about 1½ lb),
halved, pitted, and sliced

1¼ cups **raspberries**

milk, to glaze

Reserve one-third of the dough for the lattice. Roll out
the remainder on a lightly floured surface until large
enough to line the bottom and sides of a buttered
metal pie plate, 8 inches in diameter and 2 inches
deep. Lift the dough over a rolling pin, drape into the
plate, then press over the bottom and sides.

Mix the sugar, cornstarch, and lemon rind together,
then add the fruit and toss together gently. Pile into the
pie plate. Trim off the excess dough, add to the
reserved portion, then roll out. Cut into ¾ wide strips
long enough to go over the top of the pie.

Brush the top edge of the pie with milk and arrange
the pastry strips over the top as a lattice. Trim off the
excess. Brush with milk, then sprinkle with a little sugar.

Bake the pie in a preheated oven, at 375°F, for
30–35 minutes, until golden. Let cool for 15 minutes,
then serve cut into wedges, drizzled with melba sauce.

For melba sauce, to serve as an accompaniment,
put 1⅔ cups raspberries in a saucepan with the juice
of ½ lemon and 2 tablespoons confectioners' sugar,
and cook for 2–3 minutes, until the raspberries are
just tender. Cool, then puree in a blender and strain
to remove the seeds. Serve warm or cold with
wedges of pie.

deep dish citrus apple pies

Makes **12**
Preparation time **40 minutes**
Cooking time **30 minutes**

3 large **cooking apples**,
    (about 1½ lb), quartered,
    cored, peeled, and sliced
grated rind and juice of
  1 lemon
4 tablespoons **butter**
½ cup **superfine sugar**, plus
    extra for sprinkling
juice of ½ **orange**
1 tablespoon **cornstarch**
⅓ cup **golden raisins**
1½ quantities **all-butter
    sweet basic flaky pastry
    dough** (see page 10)
beaten egg or **milk**, to glaze

Toss the apple slices in the lemon rind and juice. Heat the butter in a large skillet, add the apples, sugar, and orange rind, and cook gently for 5 minutes, until the apples are softened but still hold their shape.

Mix the cornstarch with the orange juice, add to the skillet with the golden raisins, and cook until the juices have thickened. Remove from the heat and let cool.

Reserve one-third of the dough, then roll out the remainder thinly on a lightly floured surface. Stamp out twelve 4 inch circles with a plain cookie cutter and press into a buttered 12-cup muffin pan.

Spoon the apple filling into the pie shells, doming it up high in the center. Roll out the reserved dough and any dough trimmings, then cut out twelve 3 inch lids with a fluted cookie cutter. Brush the pie edges with milk, then press the lids on the pies. Reroll the trimmings and cut small decorations. Brush the tops of the pies with milk, add the decorations, and brush these with egg or milk, then sprinkle with a little superfine sugar.

Bake in a preheated oven, at 375°F, for 25 minutes, until the pastry is golden. Let stand in the pans for 20 minutes, then loosen the edges with a knife, lift out of the pans, and serve warm with custard.

For deep dish blackberry & apple pies, toss 3 sliced cooking apples (about 1¼ lb) in the grated rind and juice of 1 lemon, cook gently in 4 tablespoons butter, and sweeten with ½ cup superfine sugar until softened. Thicken the sauce with 1 tablespoon cornstarch mixed with a little water, then add 1 cup blackberries and let cool. Use to fill the pies as above.

moroccan almond spiral

Serves **8**

Preparation time **30 minutes**

Cooking time **30–35 minutes**

½ lb (2 sticks) **butter**, at room
  temperature

1 ¼ cups **superfine sugar**

3 tablespoons **honey**

2 **eggs**

2 cups **ground almonds**

2 tablespoons **all-purpose
  flour**

grated rind of 1 **lemon**

grated rind of 1 **orange**

¾ cup **walnut pieces**, finely
  chopped

4 teaspoons **rose water**

6 sheets of **phyllo pastry**,
  19 × 9 inches, defrosted
  if frozen

4 tablespoons melted **butter**,
  for brushing

sifted **confectioners' sugar**,
  for dusting

fresh or **dried rose and
  lavender petals**, to decorate

Cream the butter and sugar together. Add the honey
and gradually beat in the eggs. Stir in the ground almonds,
flour, fruit rinds, chopped walnuts, and rose water.

Unfold the pastry sheets, then arrange 5 sheets with
the long edges facing you, overlapping the short edges
slightly and sticking them together with a little melted
butter, until you have a long continuous strip, about
7 ½ feet long. Reserve the remaining pastry sheet in
case you need to mend any broken pastry later.

Spoon or pipe the almond filling about 2 inches from
the long bottom edge in a line parallel with the bottom
pastry edge. Fold the sides in to enclose the filling,
then fold up the bottom of the pastry over the filling.
Now, carefully roll up to the top edge of the pastry strip
and stick the top edge over the roll with melted butter.

Beginning at one of the farthest ends of the almond
roll, begin to coil the pastry around loosely to form a
10 inch diameter circle.

Tear the remaining pastry sheet into strips to mend
any broken areas of pastry, holding strips in place with
melted butter. Phyllo pastry dries out quickly, so try to
shape the pie as fast as you can.

Lift the pastry up and slide a baking sheet underneath
it. Bake the pastry in a preheated oven, at 350°F, for
30–35 minutes, until golden brown. Let cool, then
transfer to a cutting board, dust the pastry heavily with
confectioners' sugar, and sprinkle with dried rose petals
and lavender. Serve warm or cold, cut into wedges.

mile-high chocolate meringue pie

Serves **6**

Preparation time **40 minutes**, plus chilling

Cooking time **55–60 minutes**

For the filling

4 **eggs**, separated

¾ cup plus 2 tablespoons **superfine sugar**

3 tablespoons **unsweetened cocoa powder**, sifted

1 tablespoon **cornstarch**

1¼ cups **milk**

1 teaspoon **vanilla extract**

2 oz **semisweet dark chocolate**, grated, plus extra to decorate

For the pastry dough

¾ cup plus 2 tablespoons **all-purpose flour**

3 tablespoons **unsweetened cocoa powder**

3 tablespoons **superfine sugar**

4 tablespoons **butter**, diced

4–5 teaspoons **cold water**

Make the dough. Add the flour, cocoa, sugar, and butter to a large bowl, then rub in with your fingertips or an electric mixer until you have fine crumbs. Mix in enough water to form a soft but not sticky dough. Roll out on a floured surface to fit a loose-bottom fluted tart pan, 8 inches in diameter, 2 inches deep. Line the pan (see page 14). Prick the bottom with a fork and chill for 15 minutes. Bake the tart blind (see page 15) for 10 minutes. Remove the paper and weights and bake for another 5 minutes.

Meanwhile, beat together the egg yolks, ¼ cup of the sugar, the cocoa powder, and cornstarch in a large bowl. Pour the milk into a saucepan and bring to a boil. Gradually whisk the hot milk into the egg yolk mixture and then pour it back into the saucepan, whisking continuously until thick. Stir in the vanilla, then pour into the tart shell.

Whisk the egg whites until stiff. Gradually beat in the remaining sugar until it has all been added and the meringue is thick, then fold in the grated chocolate. Spoon the meringue over the pie, shape into swirls, then bake at at 350°F, for 15 minutes, until the meringue is golden. Cool before serving sprinkled with extra grated chocolate to decorate.

For chocolate banana cream pie, make the tart shell and fill as above, then let cool. Cover the top with 2 sliced bananas tossed in the juice of ½ lemon. Whip 1¼ cups heavy cream, flavored with 2 tablespoons confectioners' sugar and 2–3 tablespoons rum. Spoon over the top and decorate with chocolate curls.

peach & blueberry jalousie

Serves **6**
Preparation time **30 minutes**
Cooking time **20–25 minutes**

16 oz chilled **store-bought puff pastry**
4 **ripe peaches** or **nectarines**, halved, pitted, and thickly sliced
1 cup **blueberries**
¼ cup **superfine sugar**, plus a little extra for sprinkling
grated rind of ½ **lemon**
1 **egg**, beaten
confectioners' sugar, for dusting
beaten egg, to glaze

Roll out half the pastry on a lightly floured surface and trim to a 12 x 7 inch rectangle. Transfer to a lightly oiled baking sheet.

Pile the peach or nectarine slices on top, leaving a 1 inch border of pastry showing, then sprinkle on the blueberries, sugar, and lemon rind. Brush the pastry border with a little beaten egg.

Roll out the remaining pastry to a little larger than the first piece, then trim to 13 x 8 inches. Fold in half lengthwise, then make cuts in from the fold about ½ inch apart and 2½ inches long, leaving a wide uncut border of pastry.

Lift the pastry over the fruit, unfold so that the fruit and bottom layer of pastry are completely covered, then press the pastry edges together. Trim if needed. Push up the edges with a knife, then flute (see page 17).

Brush the top of the pastry with beaten egg, sprinkle with a little extra sugar, and bake in a preheated oven, at 400°F, for 20–25 minutes, until the pastry is well risen and golden brown. Dust with confectioners' sugar and serve cut into squares, warm or cold, with cream or ice cream.

For apple & blackberry jalousie, replace the peaches and blueberries with 4 Granny Smith apples, quartered, cored, and thickly sliced, and 1 cup blackberries.

gooseberry & elderflower pies

Makes **4**

Preparation time **30 minutes**

Cooking time **20–25 minutes**

⅔ cup **superfine sugar**, plus
   extra for sprinkling

2 teaspoons **cornstarch**

2⅔ cups **gooseberries**, fresh
   or canned if not in season

1 quantity **lemon-flavored
   pâte sucrée dough**, chilled
   (see page 11)

1 tablespoon **elderflower
   syrup**, undiluted

milk or **beaten egg**, to glaze

Mix together the sugar, cornstarch, and gooseberries in a bowl. Cut the dough into 4 pieces, then roll each piece out to a roughly shaped 7 inch circle. Drape each piece into a buttered individual metal tart pan, 4 inches in diameter and 1 inch deep, leaving the excess dough overhanging the edges of the pans.

Spoon in the gooseberry mixture and mound up in the center, then drizzle over the elderflower syrup. Fold the overhanging dough up and over the filling, pleating where needed and leaving the centers of the pies open.

Brush the pastry with milk or beaten egg, sprinkle with a little sugar, and bake in a preheated oven, at 375°F, for 20–25 minutes, until golden. Let stand for 15 minutes, then loosen the edges and lift the pies out of the pan. Serve with elderflower cream (see below).

For elderflower cream, to serve as an accompaniment, whip 1 cup heavy cream, then fold in 2 tablespoons undiluted elderflower syrup (sometimes labeled as elderflower cordial, available for specialty gourmet stores) and the grated rind of ½ lemon.

deep dish puff apple pie

Serves **6**
Preparation time **40 minutes**
Cooking time **20–25 minutes**

5 **cooking apples** (about
  2 lb), quartered, cored,
  peeled, and thickly sliced
½ cup **superfine sugar**, plus
  extra for sprinkling
grated rind of 1 small **orange**
½ teaspoon **ground apple pie
  spice** or **ground cinnamon**
3 whole **cloves**
13 oz chilled **store-bought
  puff pastry**
beaten egg, to glaze

Fill a 1¼ quart pie plate with the apples. Mix the sugar with the orange rind, apple pie spice or cinnamon, and cloves, then sprinkle over the apples.

Roll the pastry out on a lightly floured surface until a little larger than the top of the dish. Cut 2 long strips from the edges, about ½ inch wide. Brush the plate rim with a little beaten egg, press the strips on top, then brush these with egg (see page 16). Lift the remaining pastry over the plate and press the edges together well.

Trim off the excess dough, raise up the edges with a small knife, then flute (see pages 17). Reroll the trimmings and cut out small heart shapes or circles with a small cookie cutter. Brush the top of the pie with beaten egg, add the dough shapes, then brush these with egg. Sprinkle with a little extra sugar.

Bake the pie in a preheated oven, at 400°F, for 20–25, minutes until the pastry is well risen and golden. Serve warm with spoonfuls of crème fraîche or whipped cream.

For spiced plum & pear pie, substitute 3 sliced pears (about 1 lb) and 8 sliced plums for the apples (about 1 lb), sprinkle with ⅓ cup superfine sugar, and add 2 halved star anise, 3 cloves, and ¼ teaspoon ground cinnamon. Omit the fruit rind, then cover with the dough and continue as above.

mixed berry pies

Makes **12**
Preparation time **40 minutes**
Cooking time **30–35 minutes**

3½ cups mixed **red currants
and black currants** or all
blueberries
2 tablespoons **water**
¾ cup **superfine sugar**,
plus extra for sprinkling
1 tablespoon **cornstarch**
1½ cups **raspberries**
1¼ cups qartered small
strawberries
1½ quantities **all-butter
sweet basic flaky pastry
dough** (see page 10)
milk, to glaze

Cook the currants or blueberries with the measured water and sugar in a saucepan for 5 minutes, stirring until soft. Mix the cornstarch with a little extra water to form a smooth paste, then stir into the fruit and cook until thickened. Add the raspberries and strawberries, stir gently together, then let cool.

Reserve one-third of the dough, then roll out the remainder thinly on a lightly floured surface. Stamp out twelve 4 inch circles with a fluted cookie cutter and press into a buttered 12-cup muffin pan. Reknead and reroll the dough trimmings as needed.

Spoon the fruit into the pies. Roll out the reserved dough and any dough trimmings and cut out twelve 3 inch lids with a fluted cookie cutter. Cut a small flower, heart, or star in the center of each. Brush the top edges of the fruit-filled pies with a little milk, add the dough lids, and press the edges together well to seal.

Brush the pies with a little milk and sprinkle with sugar. Bake in a preheated oven, at 350°F, for 25–30 minutes, until golden. Let stand in the pans for 20 minutes, then loosen the edges with a knife and lift out of the pans. Serve warm with cream.

For plum & strawberry pies, cook 8 pitted and diced plums (about 1 lb) with the water and sugar as above. Thicken with the cornstarch mixed with water, then add 1⅔ cups quartered strawberries. Use to fill the pies as above.

lemon meringue pie

Serves **6**

Preparation time **40 minutes**, plus chilling

Cooking time **35–40 minutes**

12 oz chilled store-bought or homemade **sweet basic flaky pastry dough** (see page 10)

1 cup **superfine sugar**

1/3 cup **cornstarch**

grated rind and juice of 2 **lemons**

4 **eggs**, separated

about 1 cup **water**

Roll out the dough thinly on a lightly floured surface and use to line an 8 inch diameter, 2 inch deep, loose-bottom fluted tart pan, pressing evenly into the sides (see page 14). Trim the top and prick the bottom. Chill for 15 minutes. Line the tart with nonstick parchment paper, add pie weights or dried beans, and bake in a preheated oven, at 375°F, for 15 minutes. Remove the paper and weights and bake for another 5 minutes.

Put 1/3 cup of the sugar in a bowl with the cornstarch and lemon rind, add the egg yolks, and mix until smooth. Make the lemon juice up to 1 1/4 cups with the measured water, pour into a saucepan, and bring to a boil. Gradually mix into the yolk mixture, beating until smooth. Pour back into the pan and bring to a boil, beating until very thick. Pour into the pastry shell and spread level.

Whisk the egg whites until they form stiff peaks. Gradually whisk in the remaining sugar, a teaspoonful at a time, then whisk for another 1–2 minutes, until thick and glossy. Spoon over the lemon layer to cover completely and swirl with a spoon.

Reduce the oven temperature to 350°F and cook for 15–20 minutes, until the meringue is golden and cooked through. Let stand for 15 minutes, then remove the tart pan and transfer to a serving plate. Serve warm or cold with cream.

For citrus meringue pie, mix the grated rind of 1 lime, 1 lemon, and 1/2 small orange with the cornstarch. Squeeze the juice from the fruits and make up to 1 1/4 cups with water. Continue as above.

apricot & pistachio purses

Makes **8**

Preparation time **25 minutes**, plus chilling

Cooking time **15 minutes**

6 tablespoons **butter**, at room temperature

2 tablespoons **superfine sugar**

few drops of **almond extract** or **orange flower water**

1 medium **egg yolk**

¼ cup **ground almonds**

3 tablespoons coarsely chopped **pistachio nuts**

8 **apricots**

4 sheets of **phyllo pastry**, 19 × 9 inches, defrosted if frozen

sifted **confectioners' sugar**, for dusting

Cream 2 tablespoons of the butter with the sugar and almond extract or orange flower water until light and pale. Add the egg yolk and ground almonds, mix until smooth, then stir in the pistachios. Chill for 15 minutes.

Cut each apricot in half, remove the pits, then sandwich the apricots back together with the pistachio mixture in the middle.

Melt the remaining butter. Unfold the pastry sheets and put one sheet on your work surface. Brush with melted butter, then cut into 4 rectangles. Put an apricot on one of the rectangles, lift up the corners of the pastry to enclose the apricot, then pinch together at the top of the fruit. Wrap with a second pastry rectangle at right angles to the first to form a purse shape. Repeat with a second apricot and 2 more pastry rectangles, then place on a baking sheet. Continue until all apricots have been used.

Brush with a little of the remaining butter, then bake in a preheated oven, at 375°F, for 15 minutes, until golden. Dust with confectioners' sugar and serve warm or cold with scoops of vanilla ice cream.

For apple strudel purses, omit the almond extract or orange flower water and pistachios from the creamed mixture, adding an extra ¼ cup ground almonds and ¼ teaspoon ground cinnamon, then stir in 2 cored, peeled, and diced apples and ⅓ cup golden raisins. Divide the mixture among 8 rectangles of pastry, wrap the pastry around the filling, then enclose each in a second pastry rectangle and continue as above.

sweet cherry pies

Makes **6**
Preparation time **30 minutes**
Cooking time **20–25 minutes**

²/₃ cup **superfine sugar**, plus
   extra for sprinkling
1 tablespoon **cornstarch**
½ teaspoon **ground star
   anise** or **cinnamon**
2 cups just thawed **frozen
   pitted black cherries**,
   halved
1 quantity **all-butter sweet
   basic flaky pastry dough**
   (see page 10), flavored with
   grated orange rind, chilled
milk or **beaten egg**, to glaze

Mix the sugar, cornstarch, and star anise together,
then add the cherries and toss together.

Roll out two-thirds of the dough thinly on a lightly floured
surface. Use to line six 4 inch, loose-bottom fluted tart
pans, rerolling the dough trimmings as needed.

Spoon the cherry mixture into the pastry shells, and
brush the top edges with milk or beaten egg. Roll out
the reserved dough with any trimmings and cut six
4 inch circles with a fluted cookie cutter.

Add the pie lids and press the pastry edges together
to seal. Slash the tops with a knife, then brush the
tops with milk or beaten egg and sprinkle with a little
extra sugar.

Bake the pies in a preheated oven, at 350°F, for
20–25 minutes, until the pastry is golden. Let stand for
15 minutes, then loosen the edges of the pies and take
out of the pans. Serve warm or cold with custard.

For kirsch custard, to serve as an accompaniment,
whisk 3 egg yolks with 3 tablespoons superfine
sugar and 2 teaspoons cornstarch until smooth. Heat
1¼ cups milk just to boiling point, gradually whisk
into the yolks, pour back into the pan, and heat gently,
slowly bringing almost to a boil until thickened. remove
from the heat and stir in 2 tablespoons kirsch liqueur.

sweet potato meringue pie

Serves **6**

Preparation time **30 minutes**,
plus chilling

Cooking time **1 hour
5 minutes**

1 quantity **sweet basic flaky
pastry dough** (see page 10)

3 **sweet potatoes** (about
1 lb), peeled and diced

²/₃ cup **heavy cream**

¹/₃ cup firmly packed **light
brown sugar**

2 tablespoons **honey**

1 teaspoon **ground ginger**

1 teaspoon **allspice**

1 **egg**

3 **egg yolks**

For the meringue topping

3 **egg whites**

¹/₄ cup firmly packed **light
brown sugar**

¹/₄ cup **superfine sugar**

¹/₂ teaspoon **ground ginger**

Roll the pastry out on a lightly floured surface until large enough to line a buttered metal pie plate, 8 inches in diameter and 2 inches deep. Lift the dough over a rolling pin, drape into the pan, then press over the bottom and sides. Trim the edges, then chill for 15 minutes.

Put the sweet potatoes in the top of a steamer, cover, and cook for 10 minutes or until tender. Mash with the cream, sugar, honey, and spices, then beat in the whole egg and egg yolks. Pour into the pie shell, level the surface, then bake in a preheated oven, at 350°F, for 40 minutes, until set.

Make the topping. Whisk the egg whites until you have stiff peaks, then gradually whisk in the sugars, a teaspoonful at a time, until all the sugar has been added. Add the ginger and beat for an additional 1–2 minutes, until thick and glossy. Spoon over the hot pie and swirl the meringue with the back of a spoon. Bake for 15 minutes, until lightly browned and the meringue is crisp.

Let cool for 30 minutes, then cut into wedges and serve warm with scoops of vanilla ice cream.

For spiced pumpkin meringue pie, omit the sweet potato and add 4 cups peeled, seeded, and diced pumpkin instead. Steam as above, mash with the cream, spices, and egg yolks, and bake in the pie shell. Top with the meringue and return to the oven as above.

gâteau pithiviers with plums

Serves **6**
Preparation time **30 minutes**
Cooking time **25–30 minutes**

7 tablespoons **unsalted
  butter**, at room temperature
½ cup **superfine sugar**
1 cup **ground almonds**
few drops of **almond extract**
1 **egg**, beaten, plus extra
  to glaze
16 oz chilled **store-bought
  puff pastry**
6 **plums**, pitted and thickly
  sliced
sifted **confectioners' sugar**,
  for dusting

Make an almond paste. Cream together the butter and sugar in a bowl until pale and smooth. Add the almonds and almond extract, then the egg, and mix together until smooth.

Roll out half the pastry thinly on a lightly floured surface and trim to a 10 inch circle using a dinner plate as a guide. Place on a wetted baking sheet, then spread the almond paste over the top, leaving a 1 inch border of pastry around the edges. Arrange the plums in a single layer on top. Brush the pastry border with a little beaten egg.

Roll out the remaining pastry thinly and trim to a circle a little larger than the first. Cut 5 or 6 swirly S shapes out of the center of the pastry, then lift over a rolling pin and position on the almond paste. Press the edges together to seal and trim to neaten, if needed. Push up the edge to separate the pastry layers slightly, then flute (see page 17).

Brush the top with beaten egg and bake in a preheated oven, at 400°F, for 25–30 minutes, until well risen and golden. Let cool slightly, then dust the top with confectioners' sugar and serve cut into wedges with cream.

For brandied prune Pithiviers, soak 1 cup pitted prunes (dried plums) in 3 tablespoons brandy, then arrange over the almond paste instead of the plums. Continue as above.

autumnal fruit pies

Makes **6**

Preparation time **35 minutes**, plus cooling

Cooking time **45–50 minutes**

1 ¼ cups **blueberries** or **black currants**

²/₃ cup **superfine sugar**, plus extra for sprinkling

2 tablespoons **water**

1 tablespoon **cornstarch**

1 teaspoon **ground cinnamon**, plus extra for sprinkling

grated rind of 1 **orange**

6 **ripe plums**, pitted and diced

1 cup **blackberries**

milk, to glaze

For the hot water crust pastry dough

¾ cup plus 2 tablepsoons **lard**

⅓ cup **milk** mixed with ⅓ cup **water**

¼ cup **superfine sugar**

3 cups **all-purpose flour**

¼ teaspoon **salt**

Make the hot water crust pastry dough (see page 11), adding the sugar when heating the lard and milk mixture. Let cool for 20 minutes while you make the filling.

Put the blueberries, sugar, and water in a saucepan and heat for 5 minutes, until soft. Mix the cornstarch to a paste with a little water, add to the pan, and cook, stirring, until thickened. Remove from the heat and stir in the cinnamon, orange rind, plums, and blackberries. Set aside.

Reserve one-third of the warm dough, then cut the remainder into 6 pieces. Press one piece over the bottom, up, and slightly above the top of an individual 1 cup mold or ramiken. Repeat with 5 more molds.

Spoon in the filling. Cut the reserved dough into 6, then roll out each on a lightly floured surface to form lids. Cut small heart shapes in the center of each lid. Place over the filling and press the edges together well. Trim off the excess dough and flute the edges (see page 17). Brush with milk and sprinkle with extra sugar and cinnamon.

Put the molds on a baking sheet, then bake in a preheated oven, at 350°F, for 40–45 minutes, until golden. Cover with aluminum foil after 30 minutes. Let cool for 10 minutes, then serve in the molds.

For red currant & pear pies, make the dough as above. Omit the blueberries and cook 1 ½ cups red currants with the sugar and water until softened. Thicken with the cornstarch, remove from the heat, then stir in the orange rind, 2 cored, peeled, and diced pears and 1 ¼ cups raspberries in place of the plums and blackberries. Finish as above.

pumpkin pie

Serves **6**
Preparation time **30 minutes**
Cooking time **1–1¼ hours**,
 plus cooling

4 cups peeled, seeded, and
 cubed **fresh pumpkin** or
 butternut squash or
 2 (16 oz) cans **pumpkin**
3 **eggs**
½ cup firmly packed **light
 brown sugar**
2 tablespoons **all-purpose
 flour**
½ teaspoon **ground
 cinnamon**
½ teaspoon **ground ginger**
¼ teaspoon **grated nutmeg**
¾ cup plus 2 tablespoons
 milk, plus extra to glaze
14½ oz chilled store-bought
 or 1 quantity homemade
 **sweet basic flaky pastry
 dough** (see page 10)
sifted **confectioners' sugar**,
 for dusting

Cook the pumpkin or butternut squash in a covered steamer for 15–20 minutes or until tender. Cool, then puree in a liquidizer or food processor. Alternatively, skip this step if using canned pumpkin.

Beat together the eggs, sugar, flour, and spices in a bowl until just mixed. Add the pumpkin puree, beat together, then gradually mix in the milk. Set aside.

Roll out three-quarters of the dough on a lightly floured surface until large enough to line a buttered 9 inch diameter, 1 inch deep enamel pie plate. Lift the dough over a rolling pin, drape into the plate, and press over the bottom and sides. Trim off the excess and add the trimmings to the reserved pastry. Roll out thinly and cut tiny leaves, then mark veins (see page 17). Brush the pastry rim with milk, then press on the leaves around the rim, reserving a few. Put the pie on a baking sheet.

Pour the pumpkin filling into the dish, add a few leaf decorations on top of the filling, if desired, then brush these and the dish edges lightly with milk. Bake in a preheated oven, at 375°F, for 45–55 minutes, until the filling is set and the pastry cooked . Cover with foil after 20 minutes to stop the pastry edge from overbrowning.

Serve dusted with a little confectioners' sugar, with whipped cream sprinkled with a little extra ground spice, if desired.

For gingered pumpkin pie with maple syrup, omit the brown sugar and add ⅓ cup maple syrup. Omit the cinnamon and nutmeg and increase the ground ginger to 1½ teaspoons, adding 2 tablespoons finely chopped crystallized or preserved ginger.

sweet cranberry & orange pie

Serves **6–8**

Preparation time **30 minutes**, plus cooling

Cooking time **35–40 minutes**

4½ cups **cranberries** (about 1 lb)

¾ cup **superfine sugar**

grated rind and juice of **1 orange**

2 tablespoons **water**

1 tablespoon **cornstarch**

16 oz **store-bought puff pastry**, defrosted if frozen

beaten egg, to glaze

To decorate

¾ cup **confectioners' sugar**, sifted

grated rind and juice of ½ **orange**

Cook the cranberries in a saucepan with the sugar, orange rind and juice, and the measured water for 10 minutes, stirring occasionally until the cranberries are soft. Mix the cornstarch to a paste with a little extra water, add to the cranberries, and cook for a few minutes, stirring until thickened, then let cool.

Cut the pastry in half, roll out one half on a lightly floured surface, and trim to an 8 × 10 inch rectangle, then transfer to a buttered baking sheet. Brush the egg in a border around the edge of the rectangle, then pile the cranberry mixture in the middle.

Roll out the remaining pastry a little larger than the first half and drape over the cranberries. Press the pastry edges together to seal well, then trim the top pastry layer to match the lower one. Push up the edges of the pastry, then flute (see page 17).

Brush the top with egg, then bake in a preheated oven, at 400°F, for 25–30 minutes, until well risen and golden brown. Let cool for 30 minutes.

Mix the confectioners' sugar with enough of the orange juice to make a smooth icing that just falls from a spoon, drizzle over the pie to decorate, and sprinkle with the grated orange rind. Set aside for 20 minutes or until the icing is set, then cut into strips to serve.

For mixed berry pie, cook 4 cups of mixed blackberries, cherries, and blueberries with ½ cup superfine sugar and the rind and juice of 1 orange, but no extra water. Thicken with cornstarch and finish as above, dusting the top with confectioners' sugar instead of the icing.

chocolate cream pie

Serves **6–8**

Preparation time **30 minutes**,
plus chilling and cooling

Cooking time **45–50 minutes**

1 quantity **chocolate all-
butter sweet basic flaky
pastry dough**, chilled
(see pages 10), made by
replacing 2 tablespoons
flour with 3 tablespoons
cocoa powder

5 oz **semisweet dark
chocolate**, broken into
pieces

2 cups **reduced-fat cream
cheese**, softened

½ cup **superfine sugar**

1 tablespoon **all-purpose
flour**

1 teaspoon **vanilla extract**

3 **eggs**

Roll the dough out on a lightly floured surface a little
larger than a buttered 9 inch loose-bottom, fluted tart
pan 1½ inches deep. Press the dough over the bottom
and sides and trim off the excess with scissors so it
stands just above the top of the pan. Prick the bottom
with a fork, then chill for 15 minutes.

Bake the tart blind (see page 15) for 15 minutes.
Remove the paper and weights and cook for another
5 minutes. Reduce the oven temperature to 300°F.

Meanwhile, melt the chocolate in a bowl over hot water.
Put the cream cheese in a bowl, add the sugar, flour,
and vanilla extract, then gradually beat in the eggs until
smooth. Ladle about one-third into the chocolate bowl
and mix until smooth.

Pour the vanilla cheese mixture into the tart shell, then
pipe over the chocolate mixture over the top and swirl
together with the handle of a teaspoon to create a
marbled effect. Bake for 30–35 minutes, until set
around the edges, beginning to crack, and the center
still wobbles slightly. Let cool in the turned-off oven.

When cool, refrigerate overnight. Remove the pie from
the pan, put it on a plate, and serve cut into wedges.

For a vanilla cream pie, make a plain tart shell with
all-butter sweet basic flaky pastry dough, omitting the
cocoa powder. Bake blind, then fill with the vanilla
cheese mixture, omitting the melted chocolate and
adding ⅓ cup golden raisins and the grated rind of
1 lemon instead. Bake as above, then top with 1 cup
whipped heavy cream before serving.

blackberry & apple streusel pie

Serves **8–10**
Preparation time **40 minutes**,
    plus chilling
Cooking time **40–45 minutes**

3 cups **all-purpose flour**
²/₃ cup **superfine sugar**
¼ lb plus **4 tablespoons**
    (1½ sticks) **butter**, diced
½ cup **slivered almonds**
3–3½ tablespoons **cold water**
sifted **confectioners' sugar**,
    for dusting

For the filling
⅓ cup **superfine sugar**
2 teaspoons **cornstarch**
5 **cooking apples** (about 2 lb)
1⅓ cups **blackberries**

Add the flour, sugar, and butter to a large bowl and rub in with your fingertips or an electric mixer until you have fine crumbs. Divide into thirds, add the slivered almonds to one-third, and reserve this for the streusel topping.

Mix in just enough water to the remaining two-third dough crumbs to form a soft but not sticky dough. Knead lightly until smooth, then roll out on a floured surface until a little larger than a buttered 11 inch loose-bottom, fluted tart pan. Lift the dough over a rolling pin, drape into the pan, then press over the bottom and sides. Trim off the excess dough with scissors so that it stands a little above the top of the pan. Chill for 15 minutes.

Make the filling. Mix the sugar and cornstarch together. Quarter, core, and peel the apples, slice, and add to the sugar mixture with the blackberries. Toss together gently, then pile into the tart pan. Spoon the streusel mixture on top and stand the pan on a baking sheet.

Bake the pie in a preheated oven, at 375°F, for 40–45 minutes, checking after 25 minutes and covering with aluminum foil if the almonds and edge of the pastry seem to be browning too quickly. Let cool in the pan for 15 minutes, then dust the top with confectioners' sugar. Remove the pie from the pan and cut into wedges. Serve with whipped cream.

For Christmas apple & mincemeat pie, make the tart shell and streusel topping as above. Fill with 5 peeled, cored, and sliced apples, ¾ cup mincemeat, and 2 tablespoons chopped crystallized ginger. Sprinkle with the streusel topping and bake as above.

sweet tarts

minted fig tarts

Makes **12**

Preparation time **30 minutes**, plus chilling and cooling

Cooking time **9–10 minutes**

1 quantity **pâte sucrée dough** (see page 11), chilled

1¼ cups **heavy cream**

1 cup **Greek yogurt**

2 tablespoons **Greek honey**, plus extra for drizzling

¼ cup chopped **mint**

12 **figs**

tiny **mint leaves**, to decorate

Roll the dough out thinly on a lightly floured surface, then stamp out twelve 4 inch circles with a fluted cookie cutter and press into a buttered 12-cup muffin pan. Reknead and reroll the dough trimmings as needed. Prick the bottoms of each tart 2–3 times with a fork, then chill for 15 minutes.

Line the tarts with squares of nonstick parchment paper and pie weights or dried beans and bake in a preheated oven, at 375°F, for 5 minutes. Remove the paper and weights and cook for another 4–5 minutes, until golden. Let cool for 10 minutes, then loosen the edges and transfer to a wire rack to cool.

Whip the cream to form soft swirls, then fold in the yogurt, honey, and mint. Spoon into the tart shells. Cut the figs into wedges and arrange over the top of the tarts. Drizzle with extra honey and sprinkle with tiny mint leaves just before serving.

For minted plum tarts, make and fill the tarts as above, then slice 9 ripe plums and lightly sauté in 2 tablespoons butter with 1 tablespoon honey until hot. Spoon over the tarts and serve immediately.

strawberry chiffon tart

Serves **6**

Preparation time **40 minutes**,
plus chilling and cooling

Cooking time **20 minutes**

1 quantity **pâte sucrée dough**
(see page 11), chilled

6 small **strawberries** with
hulls, to decorate

For the filling

2 tablespoons **water**

1 ½ teaspoons **powdered
gelatin**

1 cup hulled and sliced
strawberries

⅔ cup **heavy cream**

⅔ cup **Greek yogurt**

2 tablespoons **confectioners'
sugar**

few drops of **vanilla extract**

For the gelatin topping

1 ½ teaspoons **powdered
gelatin**

6 tablespoons **water**

1 ½ cups hulled **strawberries**

2 tablespoons **confectioners'
sugar**

few drops of **vanilla extract**

Roll out the dough on a floured surface until a little larger than a buttered loose-bottom, fluted tart pan with sloping sides, 8 inches in diameter at the top and 2 inches deep. Press the dough over the bottom and sides and trim off the excess so it stands a little above the top of the pan. Prick the bottom with a fork, then chill for 15 minutes. Bake blind (see page 15) and let cool.

Make the filling. Add the water to a small heatproof bowl, then sprinkle over the gelatin, making sure it is completely absorbed by the water. Let rest for 5 minutes. Stand the bowl in a saucepan of gently simmering water until the gelatin has completely dissolved to a clear liquid.

Puree the strawberries, then strain. Whip the cream to form soft swirls, then fold in the yogurt, strawberry puree, sugar, and vanilla. Gradually add the dissolved gelatin, pour into the tart shell, and chill for 1 hour.

Make the gelatin topping. Sprinkle the gelatin over 2 tablespoons water and let soak as before. Add the strawberries to a saucepan with the remaining water and sugar and cook for 5 minutes, mashing until soft. Remove from the heat and stir in the gelatin until dissolved. Puree until smooth, then add the vanilla. Let cool.

Pour the gelatin over the top of the tart, add the small strawberries around the edge of the tart, and chill for 2–3 hours or until set. Remove the tart from the pan, transfer to a serving plate, and cut into portions.

For blackberry chiffon tart, make the tart shell and filling as above, using blackberries instead of the strawberries and omitting the vanilla. Add 2 tablespoons blackberry liqueur to the gelatin layer.

french apple flan

Makes **4**

Preparation time **20 minutes**,
plus chilling

Cooking time **25–30 minutes**

12 oz **store-bought puff
pastry**

2 **crisp green apples**, such
as Granny Smith, peeled,
cored, and sliced

1 tablespoon **superfine sugar**

2 tablespoons **unsalted
butter**, chilled

crème fraîche, to serve

For the apricot glaze

¾ cup **apricot preserves**

2 teaspoons **lemon juice**

2 teaspoons **water**

Cut the pastry into 4, then roll out each piece on
a lightly floured surface until ⅛ inch thick. Cut out
4 circles using a 5½ inch plate as a guide—instead of
making a continuous cut, which can stretch the dough,
make a number of short cuts around the plate with a
knife. Place on a baking sheet.

Place a slightly smaller plate on each pastry circle and
score around the edge to form a ½ inch border. Prick
the centers with a fork and chill for 30 minutes.

Arrange the apple slices in a circle over the pastry
circles and sprinkle with the sugar. Grate the butter
over the top. Bake in a preheated oven, at 425°F, for
25–30 minutes, until the pastry and apples are golden.

Meanwhile, make the apricot glaze. Put the preserves
in a small saucepan with the lemon juice and the
measured water and heat gently until the preserves
melt. Increase the heat and boil for 1 minute, remove
from the heat, and press through a fine strainer. Keep
warm, then brush over each apple tart while they are
still warm. Serve with ice cream.

For peach tarts, replace the 2 apples with 2 peaches,
halved, skinned, and thinly sliced. Arrange on the
pastry circles and continue as above, baking for
12–15 minutes.

classic lemon tart

Serves **8**

Preparation time **20 minutes**,
plus chilling

Cooking time **40–45 minutes**

3 **eggs**

1 **egg yolk**

2 cups **heavy cream**

½ cup **sugar**

⅔ cup **lemon juice**

For the pastry dough

1⅔ cups **all-purpose flour**

½ teaspoon **salt**

7 tablespoons **butter**, diced

2 tablespoons **confectioners'
sugar**, plus extra for dusting

2 **egg yolks**

1–2 teaspoons **cold water**

Make the pastry dough. Put the flour and salt in a mixing bowl, add the butter, and rub in with your fingertips or using an electric mixer until you have fine crumbs.

Stir in the confectioners' sugar and gradually work in the egg yolks and the measured water to form a firm dough.

Knead the dough briefly on a lightly floured surface, then wrap with plastic wrap and chill for 30 minutes. Roll out the dough and use to line a 10 inch fluted pie plate or tart pan. Prick the tart shell with a fork and chill for 20 minutes.

Line the tart shell with nonstick parchment paper and pie weights or dried beans and bake in a preheated oven, at 400°F, for 10 minutes. Remove the paper and weights and bake for another 10 minutes, until crisp and golden. Remove from the oven and reduce the oven temperature to 300°F.

Beat together all the filling ingredients, pour them into the tart shell, and bake for 20–25 minutes or until the filling is just set. Let the tart cool completely, dust with sifted confectioners' sugar, and serve.

For dark chocolate tart, make the tart shell as above and bake blind. Heat 2 cups heavy cream in a saucepan with 5 oz semisweet dark chocolate, stirring until the chocolate has melted. Beat 3 eggs and 1 egg yolk with ¼ cup superfine sugar and ¼ teaspoon ground cinnamon. Gradually beat in the chocolate cream. Bake as above and serve cold, dusted with sifted unsweetened cocoa powder.

double chocolate & hazelnut tarts

Makes **6**
Preparation time **30 minutes**,
  plus chilling and cooling
Cooking time **12 minutes**

1 quantity **pâte sucrée
  dough with hazelnuts** (see
  page 11), chilled
8 oz **semisweet dark
  chocolate**, broken into
  pieces
1 tablespoon **butter**
3 **eggs**, separated
1½ cups **heavy cream**
2 tablespoons **confectioners'
  sugar**
4 oz **white chocolate**, broken
  into pieces
4 teaspoons **kahlua** or **Irish
  cream liqueur**
2 oz **milk chocolate**, melted,
  for drizzling

Cut the dough into 6 pieces, then roll each piece out thinly on a lightly floured surface until a little larger than a buttered 4 inch individual, loose-bottom fluted tart pan. Press the dough over the bottom and sides, then trim with scissors to a little above the top of the pan. Repeat until 6 tart shells have been made. Put on a baking sheet, prick the bottoms with a fork, then chill for 15 minutes. Bake the tarts blind (see page 15) for 8 minutes, remove the paper and weights, and cook for another 4 minutes, until golden. Let cool.

Melt the dark chocolate and butter in a bowl set over a saucepan of gently simmering water, making sure that the water does not touch the bottom of the bowl. Stir in the egg yolks, one by one, then take the bowl off the heat and stir in ⅓ cup of the cream and the sugar.

Whisk the egg whites until they form soft peaks, then fold a tablespoon into the chocolate mixture to loosen it. Add the remaining egg whites and fold in gently. Pour into the baked tart shells and chill for 3 hours, until set.

Melt the white chocolate in a bowl over hot water as above. Remove the tarts from the pans and transfer to serving plates. Whip the remaining cream until it forms soft swirls, fold in the white chocolate and liqueur, then spoon onto the tarts. Drizzle with the milk chocolate and let stand for 10 minutes before serving.

For double chocolate & orange tarts, add the grated rind of 1 orange to the dough. Make and bake the tarts as above, then fill with the chocolate mousse. When set, top with white chocolate cream flavored with 4 teaspoons Grand Marnier or Cointreau.

apricot tarts

Serves **4**

Preparation time **15 minutes**

Cooking time **20–25 minutes**

12 oz **store-bought puff pastry**, defrosted if frozen

⅓ cup **marzipan**

12 **canned apricot halves**, drained

light brown sugar, for sprinkling

apricot preserves, to glaze

Cut 4 circles from the pastry using a saucer as a template, each approximately 3½ inches in diameter. Score a line about ½ inch from the edge of each circle with a sharp knife.

Roll out the marzipan to ¼ inch thick and cut out 4 circles to fit inside the scored circles. Lay the pastry circles on a baking sheet, place a circle of marzipan in the center of each, and arrange 3 apricot halves, cut side up, on top. Sprinkle a little sugar into each apricot.

Put the baking sheet on top of a second preheated baking sheet (this helps to make the bottom of the pastry more crispy) and bake in a preheated oven, at 400°F, for 20–25 minutes, until the pastry is puffed and browned and the apricots are slightly caramelized around the edges. While still hot, brush the tops with apricot preserves to glaze. Serve immediately.

For banana tarts with rum mascarpone, follow the recipe above, but use 2 thickly sliced bananas in place of the apricots. While the tarts are baking, in a bowl, mix together ¼ cup mascarpone cheese, 2 tablespoons rum, and 2 tablespoons light brown sugar. Spoon on top of the hot tarts and serve immediately.

tarte tatin with mulled pears

Serves **6**

Preparation time **30 minutes**, plus cooling

Cooking time **45 minutes**

4 tablespoons **butter**

¾ cup **superfine sugar**

¾ cup plus 2 tablespoons **red wine**

1 **cinnamon stick**, broken in half

2 **star anise**

3 **cloves**

6 **Bosc pears** (about 1½ lb), halved, peeled, and cored

few drops of **red food coloring** (optional)

8 oz **store-bought puff pastry**, defrosted if frozen

Melt the butter in a large skillet, add the sugar, wine, and spices and heat gently until the sugar has dissolved.

Add the pears to the red wine mixture and simmer, turning occasionally, for about 5 minutes, until the pears are almost tender and evenly colored. Scoop out of the skillet and set aside.

Increase the heat and simmer the mixture for 5 minutes or until it is reduced and syrupy. Turn off the heat, stir in the food coloring, if using, then return the pears to the skillet and coat in the syrup. Let cool for 15 minutes.

Roll out the pastry on a lightly floured surface, then trim to a 10 inch circle. Transfer the pears, syrup, and spices to a buttered metal pie plate, 8 inches in diameter and 2 inches deep. Lay the pastry on top, tucking it down the sides of the pan Make 4 small steam vents in the top with a knife, then bake (unglazed) in a preheated oven, at 400°F, for 30 minutes, until the pastry is risen, has shrunk from the sides of the pan, and the juices are bubbling.

Let stand for 5 minutes. Loosen the edges with a knife, cover with a large serving plate, then invert the pan.

For apple tarte tatin with applejack, heat
6 tablespoons butter in a skillet with ¾ cup superfine sugar until the sugar dissolves, then increase the heat and cook for 3–5 minutes, without stirring, until golden. Meanwhile, quarter, core, and peel 6 firm apples, toss in the juice of 1 lemon, add to the syrup, and cook gently for 10 minutes. Cool, add to the pie plate, cover with pastry, and bake as above. Turn out, and serve topped with ¼ cup warmed applejack flamed with a match.

italian ricotta tarts

Makes **12**
Preparation time **20 minutes**,
Cooking time **15–20 minutes**

8 oz **store-bought puff
  pastry**, defrosted if frozen
½ cup **ricotta cheese**
1 **egg**
¼ cup **superfine sugar**
grated rind of ½ **orange**
1 tablespoon chopped
  candied peel
2 oz **semisweet dark
  chocolate**, diced
½ cup diced **dried apricots**
¼ cup chopped **candied
  cherries**
sifted **confectioners' sugar**,
  for dusting

Roll out the pastry thinly on a lightly floured surface, then stamp out twelve 3¼ inch circles with a plain cookie cutter and press into a buttered 12-cup muffin pan. Prick the bottom of each 2–3 times with a fork.

Mix the ricotta, egg, and sugar together in a bowl until smooth, then stir in the orange rind, candied peel, diced chocolate, and fruit.

Spoon into the pastry shells and bake in a preheated oven, at 375°F, for 15–20 minutes, until well risen and the tops of the tarts are golden. Let stand for 5 minutes, then loosen the edges with a knife and transfer to a wire rack. Dust with confectioners' sugar and let cool before serving.

For English curd tarts, mix ½ cup cream cheese with 1 egg and ¼ cup superfine sugar, then stir in the grated rind of 1 lemon, 2 tablespoons chopped candied peel, and ⅔ cup golden raisins. Bake as above, then dust with confectioners' sugar.

cherry frangipane tart

Serves **8**

Preparation time **35 minutes**,
  plus chilling

Cooking time **50 minutes**

14½ oz chilled store-bought or
  homemade **sweet basic
  flaky pastry dough** (see
  page 10)

1⅔ cups pitted **fresh
  cherries** or 1 (14 oz) can,
  drained

3 **eggs**

½ cup **superfine sugar**

6 tablespoons **unsalted
  butter**, melted

few drops of **almond extract**

1 cup **ground almonds**

2 tablespoons **slivered
  almonds**

sifted **confectioners' sugar**,
  for dusting

Roll out the dough on a lightly floured surface until large enough to line a buttered 10 inch deep, loose-bottom fluted tart pan. Lift the dough over a rolling pin, drape into the pan, and press it over the bottom and sides. Trim off excess dough with scissors so that it stands a little above the top of the pan. Prick the bottom of the tart with a fork, then chill for 15 minutes.

Line the tart shell with nonstick parchment paper, add pie weights or dried beans, and bake blind in a preheated oven, at 375°F, for 15 minutes. Remove the paper and weights and cook for another 5 minutes. Reduce the oven temperature to 350°F.

Arrange the cherries in the bottom of the tart. Beat the eggs and sugar together until thick and the beaters or whisk leave a trail when lifted out of the mixture. Gently fold in the melted butter and almond extract, then the ground almonds. Pour the mixture over the cherries and sprinkle with the slivered almonds.

Cook the tart for 30 minutes, until golden brown and the filling is set. Check after 20 minutes and cover the top loosely with aluminum foil if the tart seems to be browning too quickly.

Let cool in the pan for 30 minutes, then remove and dust with sifted confectioners' sugar before serving.

For cherry, almond & jam tart, make the tart shell and bake blind as above, then spread ¼ cup strawberry or raspberry jam over the shell. Add the almond mixture and slivered almonds and bake as above.

178

glazed linzer torte

Serves **8**

Preparation time **30 minutes**,
  plus chilling and cooling

Cooking time **25–30 minutes**

1³/₄ cups **red currants**

juice of ½ **lemon**

½ cup **superfine sugar**

2 tablespoons **cornstarch**,
  mixed with a little water to
  form a paste

2½ cups **raspberries**

1 tablespoon **red currant jelly**
  or **raspberry jelly**

For the pastry dough

1¹/₃ cups plus 1 tablespoon
  all-purpose flour

7 tablespoons **butter**, diced

¹/₃ cup **confectioners' sugar**

¹/₃ cup plus 1 tablespoon
  ground almonds

grated rind of 1 **lemon**

2 **egg yolks**

Make the dough. Add the flour and butter to a bowl and rub in with your fingertips or an electric mixer until you have fine crumbs. Stir in the confectioners' sugar, almonds, and lemon rind, then the egg yolks, and mix to form a dough. Chill for 15 minutes.

Knead the dough, then cut off and reserve a quarter. Roll out the remainder thinly on a lightly floured surface to fit a buttered 9½ inch, loose-bottom fluted tart pan. Press the dough over the bottom and sides of the pan. Trim off the excess and add the trimmings to the reserved dough. Chill the tart and trimmings for 15 minutes.

Add the red currants, lemon juice, and sugar to a saucepan and simmer for 5 minutes, until the fruit is soft. Stir in the cornstarch paste and cook over high heat, stirring until the fruit compote thickens. Let cool.

Spread the compote over the tart bottom, then sprinkle the raspberries over the top. Brush the shell edge with water. Roll out the trimmings and cut into ½ inch wide strips and arrange as a lattice over the tart, pressing the edges but not trimming off the excess.

Bake the tart on a baking sheet in a preheated oven, at 375°F, for 25–30 minutes, until the pastry is golden and the bottom is cooked. Trim off the excess pastry from the lattice. Warm the jelly in a small saucepan on the stove or in the microwave and brush over the pastry lattice, then let cool. Remove the tart from the pan, transfer to a serving plate, and serve.

For blackberry tart, make the tart as above, adding blueberries instead of red currants for the compote, and finishing with blackberries instead of raspberries. Dust with confectioners' sugar instead of the glaze.

blueberry & lime tarts

Makes **6**

Preparation time **30 minutes**,
 plus chilling and cooling

Cooking time **14–15 minutes**

1 quantity **pâte sucrée dough**
 (see page 11), chilled

²⁄₃ cup **heavy cream**

1 ¼ cups **canned condensed
 milk**, chilled

grated rind of 2 **limes**
 and ¼ cup **lime juice**

1 tablespoon **cornstarch**

1 tablespoon **water**

1 ⅓ cups **blueberries**

¼ cup **superfine sugar**

Cut the dough into 6 pieces, then roll each piece out thinly on a lightly floured surface until a little larger than a buttered 4 inch loose-bottom fluted tart pan. Lift into the pans, press over the bottom and sides, then trim the excess dough with scissors so it stands a little above the top of the pan. Put on a baking sheet, prick the bottoms with a fork, then chill for 15 minutes.

Line the tarts with nonstick parchment paper and pie weights or dried beans and bake blind in a preheated oven, at 375°F, for 8 minutes, then remove the paper and weights and cook for another 4 minutes, until golden. Let cool.

Beat the cream in a bowl until it foms soft swirls. Add the condensed milk and lime rind and beat to mix. Gradually beat in the lime juice until thick. Spoon into the tart shells and chill until ready to serve.

Mix the cornstarch and the measured water to a smooth paste in the bottom of a small saucepan, add the blueberries and sugar, and cook for 2–3 minutes, until the blueberries just begin to soften and the juices run. Let cool.

When ready to serve, remove the tarts from the pans and spoon the blueberry compote on top.

For Florida lime tarts, make the tart shells as above. Fill with the condensed milk, lime juice, and cream mixture, but reserve the lime rind. Chill as above. Top with ²⁄₃ cup whipped heavy cream and sprinkle with the reserved lime rind.

candied orange & chocolate tart

Serves **8**

Preparation time **35 minutes**, plus chilling and cooling

Cooking time **1¼ hours**

1 cup **superfine sugar**

¼ cup **water**

2 medium **oranges**, thinly sliced

1 quantity **all-butter sweet basic flaky pastry dough** (see page 10)

7 tablespoons **butter**, at room temperature

1 cup **ground almonds**

2 **eggs**, beaten

4 oz **semisweet dark chocolate**, melted

Add half the sugar and the water to a saucepan and heat gently until the sugar has dissolved. Add the orange slices and cook over low heat for 30 minutes, until the oranges are tender, the peel is soft and almost translucent, and most of the syrup has evaporated. Cool.

Roll the dough out thinly on a lightly floured surface to fit a buttered 9½ inch loose-bottom fluted tart pan. Press the dough over the bottom and sides of the pan. Trim off the excess with scissors so that it stands a little above the top of the pan. Chill for 15 minutes.

Bake the tart blind (see page 15) for 10 minutes. Remove the paper and weights and cook for another 5 minutes. Remove from the oven and reduce the oven temperature to 350°F.

Cream the butter and the remaining sugar in a bowl until light and fluffy. Add the ground almonds, gradually beat in the eggs until smooth, then set aside.

Reserve 10 of the best orange slices for decoration, then drain and chop the rest. Stir the melted chocolate into the almond mixture, then mix in the chopped oranges. Spread into the tart shell, arrange the reserved orange slices in a ring on top, and bake for 30 minutes. Let cool for 30 minutes before removing from the pan.

For pear & chocolate tart, make the almond mixture as above, stir in the melted chocolate, then add 4 teaspoons finely chopped crystallized ginger instead of the chopped orange. Spread it in the tart shell, then peel, core, and slice 2 pears and press these on top. Sprinkle with 2 tablespoons slivered almonds. Bake as above, then sprinkle with diced chocolate to decorate.

gingered english treacle tart

Serves **8**
Preparation time **30 minutes**
Cooking time **45–55 minutes**

2¾ cups **golden syrup** or
   light corn syrup
2 tablespoons **butter**
juice of 1 **lemon**
2¾ cups **fresh bread crumbs**
3 tablespoons drained and
   chopped **candied** or
   preserved ginger
2 **Braeburn apples**, cored
   and coarsely grated

For the pastry dough
1⅔ cups **all-purpose flour**
7 tablespoons **butter**, diced
finely grated rind of 1 **lemon**
2 tablespoons **cold water**
milk, to glaze

Put the golden syrup into a saucepan, add the butter, and heat gently until melted. Stir in the lemon juice, bread crumbs, ginger, and apples, then let cool.

Make the dough. Put the flour, butter, and lemon rind in a bowl and rub in the butter until you have fine crumbs. Mix in just enough of the measured water to form a smooth dough. Knead lightly, roll out on a lightly floured surface, and use to line a 9½ inch loose-bottom tart pan. Trim off the excess dough and reserve.

Pour the syrup mixture into the tart shell. Roll out the dough trimmings thinly, cut narrow strips, and arrange in a lattice, sticking the edges with a little milk. Brush all the strips with milk.

Place the tart on a hot baking sheet and bake in a preheated oven, at 375°F, for 40–50 minutes, until golden and the filling has set. Check after 30 minutes and cover the top loosely with aluminum foil if the tart seems to be browning too quickly.

Serve warm or cold with whipped cream or ice cream.

For pecan pie, make the tart shell as above. Warm ¾ cup light corn syrup in a saucepan with 1 cup firmly packed light brown sugar and 6 tablespoons butter until melted. Cool slightly, then beat in 3 eggs and ½ teaspoon vanilla extract. Pour into the tart shell and arrange 1¾ cups pecans on top. Bake at at 350°F, for 40–50 minutes or until set, covering with aluminum foil if the pastry seems to be browning too quickly.

pear & almond tart

Serves **8**

Preparation time **20 minutes**, plus chilling

Cooking time **50–55 minutes**

14½ oz chilled store-bought or homemade **sweet basic flaky pastry dough** (see page 10)

¼ lb (1 stick) **unsalted butter**, at room temperature

⅔ cup **superfine sugar**

1¼ cups **ground almonds**

2 **eggs**, lightly beaten

1 tablespoon **lemon juice**

3 **ripe pears**, peeled, cored, and thickly sliced

¼ cup **slivered almonds**

sifted **confectioners' sugar**, for dusting

Roll out the dough on a lightly floured surface until a little larger than a 10 inch tart pan. Lift the dough over a rolling pin, drape into the pan, then press over the bottom and sides. Trim off excess dough with scissors so that it stands a little above the top of the pan. Prick the bottom with a fork and chill for 30 minutes.

Line the tart with nonstick parchment paper, add pie weights or dried beans, and bake in a preheated oven, at 375°F, for 15 minutes. Remove the parchment paper and weights and bake for another 5–10 minutes, until the pastry is crisp and golden. Let cool completely. Reduce the oven temperature to 350°F.

Beat the butter, sugar, and ground almonds together until smooth, then beat in the eggs and lemon juice.

Arrange the pear slices over the pastry shell and carefully spread over the almond mixture. Sprinkle with the slivered almonds and bake for 30 minutes, until the topping is golden and firm to the touch. Remove from the oven and let cool.

Dust the tart with sifted confectioners' sugar and serve in wedges with chocolate sauce (see below) and some vanilla ice cream.

For chocolate sauce, to serve as an accompaniment, melt 4 oz semisweet dark chocolate, broken into pieces with 4 tablespoons unsalted butter, diced, and 1 tablespoon light corn syrup in a saucepan over a gentle heat. Let cool slightly.

toffeed apple tarts

Makes **12**
Preparation time **40 minutes**,
  plus chilling
Cooking time **20 minutes**

1 quantity **pâte sucrée dough**
  (see page 11), chilled
2 teaspoons **cornstarch**
2 tablespoons **water**
3 large **apples** (about 1½ lb),
  cored, peeled, and diced
½ cup firmly packed **light
  brown sugar**
2 tablespoons **butter**

For the topping
1 cup **heavy cream**
3 tablespoons **light brown
  sugar**

Roll the dough out thinly on a lightly floured surface, then stamp out twelve 4 inch circles with a fluted cookie cutter and press into a buttered 12-cup muffin pan, rerolling the dough trimmings as needed. Prick the bottoms 2–3 times, then chill for 15 minutes.

Bake the tarts blind (see page 15) for 5 minutes. Remove the paper and weights and cook for another 4–5 minutes, until pale golden. Remove from the oven and reduce the oven temperature to 350°F.

Meanwhile, mix the cornstarch and the measured water to a paste in a saucepan, add the apples and sugar, and cook for 10 minutes, stirring occasionally, until the butter and apples are soft. Let cool for 15 minutes, loosen the tarts, and remove from the pan.

Spoon the apples into the tart shells. Whip the cream to form soft swirls. Fold in 2 tablespoons sugar, spoon over the tarts, and sprinkle with the remaining sugar. Serve cold.

For toffee marshmallow tarts, make the tart shells and filling as above. Beat 3 egg whites until stiff, then gradually beat in ¼ cup superfine sugar and ¼ cup firmly packed light brown sugar until the meringue is thick and glossy. Spoon over the apple-filled tarts, then bake in a preheated oven, at 325°F, for 15 minutes, until browned.

double chocolate tart

Serves **6–8**
Preparation time **40 minutes**,
    plus chilling and cooling
Cooking time **40 minutes**

13 oz chilled **store-bought**
    or **homemade sweet basic**
    flaky pastry dough (see
    page 10)
5 oz **semisweet dark**
    chocolate, broken into
    pieces, plus 2 oz to decorate
5 oz **white chocolate**
7 tablespoons **unsalted**
    butter
3 **eggs**
1 **egg yolk**
½ cup **superfine sugar**
2 tablespoons **heavy cream**

Roll out the dough on a lightly floured surface until
large enough to line a buttered 9½ inch loose-bottom
fluted tart pan. Lift over a rolling pin, drape into the pan,
and press over the bottom and sides. Trim off the
excess dough, prick the bottom with a fork, then chill
for 15 minutes. Line with nonstick parchment paper, add
pie weights or dried beans, and bake in a preheated
oven, at 375°F, for 15 minutes. Remove the paper and
weights and bake for another 5 minutes. Remove from
the oven and reduce the oven temperature to 325°F.

Melt the dark and white chocolate in separate bowls
over a saucepan of simmering water. Add three-
quarters of the butter to the dark chocolate and
the rest to the white chocolate. Heat until melted.

Beat the eggs, egg yolk, and sugar in a third bowl
for 3–4 minutes, until doubled in volume (but not so
thick that the beaters or whisk leave a trail). Fold two-
thirds into the dark chocolate mixture, then pour into
the cooked tart shell. Fold the cream into the white
chocolate to loosen it, then fold in the remaining egg
mixture. Spoon over the dark chocolate layer to
completely cover. Cook the tart for 20 minutes, until
just set with a slight wobble to the center. Cool for at
least 1 hour. Pipe double lines of melted dark chocolate
and let stand for at least 30 minutes before serving.

For dark chocolate tart, melt 10 oz semisweet dark
chocolate with 7 tablespoons butter. Beat the eggs
and sugar as above and fold into the chocolate
mixture. Pour into the baked tart shell and cook for
15 minutes. Dust with sifted cocoa to serve.

mango & palm sugar tatin

Serves **8**

Preparation time **40 minutes**,
  plus freezing

Cooking time **20–25 minutes**

6 tablespoons **unsalted
  butter**

⅓ cup **palm sugar**, grated,
  or firmly packed **light brown
  sugar**

½ teaspoon ground **allspice**

3 small **mangoes**, peeled,
  pitted, and thickly sliced

12 oz chilled **store-bought
  puff pastry** or **homemade
  basic flaky pastry dough**
  (see page 9)

Make the topping. Heat the butter, sugar, and spice together in a 9 inch ovenproof skillet until the butter has melted. Remove the skillet from the heat. Carefully arrange the mango slices in the skillet, fanning them from the center outward, to make 2 layers.

Roll out the dough on a lightly floured surface a little larger than the size of the skillet. Drape it over the mangoes and press it down and around the edges of the skillet, then pierce a small hole in the center. Bake in a preheated oven, at 425°F, for 20–25 minutes, until the pastry is risen and golden. Let stand for 10 minutes before turning out on to a large plate. Serve with ice cream.

For coconut ice cream, to accompany the tatin, bring 1¼ cups whole milk, 1 (14 fl oz) can coconut milk, and 2 star anise just to a boil in a saucepan. Remove from the heat and let steep for 20 minutes, then strain. Beat 5 egg yolks with ⅓ cup superfine sugar until pale and creamy. Stir in the cream mixture, then pour back into the pan and heat gently, stirring until it coats the back of the spoon. Cool, then freeze in an electric ice-cream machine until thick or in a plastic container in the freezer, beating several times every few hours until firm.

mixed berry tarts

Makes **12**
Preparation time **30 minutes**,
  plus chilling
Cooking time **12 minutes**

1 quantity **pâte sucrée dough**
  (see page 11), chilled
1 1/4 cups **heavy cream**
1/4 cup **lemon curd**
3 tablespoons **red currant
  jelly** or **grape jelly**
juice of 1/2 **lemon**
1 2/3 cups halved or sliced
  small **strawberries**,
  depending on size
1 2/3 cups **raspberries**
1 cup **blueberries**

Roll the dough out thinly on a lightly floured surface,
then stamp out twelve 4 inch circles with a fluted
cookie cutter and press into a buttered 12-cup muffin
pan. Reknead and reroll the dough trimmings as
needed. Prick the bottoms 2–3 times with a fork,
then chill for 15 minutes.

Line the tarts with small squares of nonstick parchment
paper and pie weights or dried beans and bake in a
preheated oven, at 375°F, for 8 minutes. Remove the
paper and weights and cook for another 4–5 minutes,
until golden. Let cool for 10 minutes, then loosen the
edges and transfer to a wire rack to cool completely.

Whip the cream until it forms soft swirls, then fold in
the lemon curd. Spoon into the tart shells and spread
into an even layer with the back of a teaspoon.

Warm the red currant or raspberry jelly and lemon juice
together in a small saucepan, stirring, until the jelly has
dissolved completely. Add the fruits and toss together.
Spoon over the tarts, piling the fruit up high, then
transfer to a serving plate.

For mixed berry & white chocolate tarts, omit the
lemon curd from the cream and fold in 4 oz melted
white chocolate instead. Spoon into the tarts, arrange
the raw berries on top without the jelly glaze, then
drizzle 3 oz melted white chocolate in lines over
the fruit.

pecan, maple syrup & choc tart

Serves **8**

Preparation time **20 minutes**,
plus chilling and cooling

Cooking time **1 hour
10 minutes**

¼ lb (1 stick) **unsalted butter**,
at room temperature

½ cup firmly packed **light
brown sugar**

2 **eggs**, beaten

¼ cup **all-purpose flour**

pinch of **salt**

¾ cup **maple syrup**

1¾ cups **pecans**, toasted

¾ cup **pine nuts**, lightly
toasted

2 oz **semisweet dark
chocolate**, chopped

For the pastry dough

1⅔ cups **all-purpose flour**,
sifted

¼ teaspoon **salt**

7 tablespoons **unsalted
butter**, diced

1 **egg**, lightly beaten

2–3 teaspoons **cold water**

Make the dough. Add the flour, salt, and butter to a
bowl, then rub the butter in with your fingertips or an
electric mixer until you have fine crumbs. Add the egg
and water and continue mixing until the dough just
starts to come together. Transfer to a lightly floured
surface and knead gently. Wrap the dough in plastic
wrap and chill for 30 minutes.

Roll out the dough thinly on a lightly floured surface
and use it to line a 9 inch square tart pan (see page 14).
Prick the bottom with a fork and chill for 20 minutes.
Line the tart shell with nonstick parchment paper
add pie weights or dried beans, and bake blind in a
preheated oven, at 375°F, for 15 minutes. Remove the
paper and weights and bake for another 5–10 minutes,
until crisp and golden. Let cool. Reduce the oven
temperature to at 350°F.

Cream the butter and sugar until pale and light, then
gradually beat in the eggs, adding the flour and salt as
you work until evenly combined. Stir in the syrup (the
mixture may appear to curdle at this stage), nuts, and
chocolate and spoon the mixture into the pastry shell.

Bake for 40–45 minutes, until golden and just firm in
the center. Remove from the oven and let cool. Serve
warm with ice cream.

For traditional pecan pie, add a large pinch of
ground allspice to the dough. Use 2½ cups pecans
and omit the pine nuts and chocolate, flavoring with
1 teaspoon vanilla extract instead.

kaffir lime tart

Serves **8**

Preparation time **20 minutes**,
  plus chilling

Cooking time **33–40 minutes**

13 oz chilled store-bought or
  homemade **sweet basic
  flaky pastry dough** (see
  page 10)

a little **flour**, for dusting

¾ cup **superfine sugar**

¾ cup plus 2 tablespoons
  freshly squeezed **lime juice**
  (4–6 limes)

8 **kaffir lime leaves** or the
  grated rind of 3 **limes**

3 **eggs**

2 **egg yolks**

¼ lb plus 4 tablespoons
  (1½ sticks) **unsalted butter**,
  at room temperature

sifted **confectioners' sugar**,
  for dusting

Roll out the dough on a lightly floured surface a little larger than a 9 inch fluted tart pan. Lift the dough over a rollng pin, drape into the pan and press over the bottom and sides. Trim off any excess dough, and prick the bottom with a fork. Chill for 30 minutes.

Line the tart with nonstick parchment paper, add pie weights or dried beans, and bake in a preheated oven, at 400°F, for 15 minutes. Remove the paper and weights and bake for another 12–15 minutes, until the pastry is crisp and golden. Let cool.

Put the sugar, lime juice, and kaffir lime leaves or lime rind in a saucepan and heat gently to dissolve the sugar. Bring to a boil and simmer for 5 minutes. Let cool for 5 minutes, then strain into a clean pan.

Stir in the eggs, egg yolks, and half the butter and heat gently, stirring, for 1 minute or until the sauce coats the back of the spoon. Add the remaining butter and beat continuously until the mixture thickens.

Transfer the lime mixture to the pastry shell and bake for 6–8 minutes, until set. Let cool and serve warm dusted with confectioners' sugar.

For mango & kiwi salad to serve with the tart, peel, pit, and dice 1 large mango, then mix with 3 peeled and sliced kiwis, the seeds scooped from 3 passion fruits, and the juice of 1 lime.

macadamia & vanilla tart

Serves **8-10**
Preparation time **30 minutes**
Cooking time **45 minutes**

13 oz chilled store-bought or
   homemade **sweet basic
   flaky pastry dough** (see
   page 10)
1/3 cup firmly packed **light
   brown sugar**
2/3 cup **maple syrup**
6 tablespoons **unsalted
   butter**
1 teaspoon **vanilla extract**
1 1/2 cups **ground almonds**
4 **eggs**, beaten
1 1/3 cups coarsely chopped
   macadamia nuts

Roll out the dough thinly on a lightly floured surface a little larger than a 9 inch loose-bottom tart pan. Lift the dough over a rollng pin, drape into the pan, and press over the bottom and sides. Trim off any excess dough, and prick the bottom with a fork.

Line the tart with nonstick parchment paper, add pie weights or dried beans, and bake in a preheated oven, at 375°F, for 15 minutes. Remove the paper and weights and bake for another 5 minutes. Remove from the oven and reduce the oven temperature to 325°F.

Heat the sugar, maple syrup, and butter gently until melted. Remove from the heat and beat in the vanilla extract and ground almonds, followed by the eggs. Add half the macadamia nuts and turn the mixture into the tart shell.

Sprinkle with the remaining macadamia nuts and bake for about 25 minutes or until the filling forms a crust but remains soft underneath. Let cool for 10 minutes, then serve with ice cream or cream.

For pine nut & honey tart, make and bake the tart shell as above. Cream together 7 tablespoons unsalted butter with 1/2 cup superfine sugar. Beat in 3 eggs, one at a time, then mix in 3/4 cup warmed flower honey, the grated rind and juice of 1 lemon, and 1 1/2 cups pine nuts. Pour into the tart shell and bake in a preheated oven, at 350°F, for about 40 minutes, until browned and set.

honeyed pecan pie

Serves **8**

Preparation time **30 minutes**,
  plus chilling

Cooking time **40–45 minutes**

1 quantity **all-butter sweet
  basic flaky pastry dough**
  (see page 10)

1 cup **honey**

1 cup firmly packed **light
  brown sugar**

6 tablespoons **butter**

¼ teaspoon **ground
  cinnamon**

1 teaspoon **vanilla extract**

3 **eggs**

1½ cups **pecans**

Roll the dough out thinly on a lightly floured surface until a little larger than a buttered loose-bottom fluted tart pan, 9 inches in diameter and 1 inch deep. Line the pan with the dough (see page 14). Trim off the excess dough with scissors so that it stands a little above the top of the pan. Prick the bottom with a fork, then chill for 15 minutes.

Line the pie shell with nonstick parchment paper and pie weights and bake blind (see page 15) for 10 minutes. Remove the paper and weights and cook for another 5 minutes, until the shell is crisp. Remove from the oven and reduce the oven temperature to 350°F.

Meanwhile, put the honey, sugar, butter, and cinnamon into a saucepan and heat gently, stirring occasionally, until melted. Remove from the heat and let cool slightly.

Beat the vanilla with the eggs in a small bowl, then gradually beat into the cooled honey mixture. Pour into the pie shell and arrange the nuts over the top. Carefully transfer to the oven and bake for 25–30 minutes, until the filling is set and the nuts have darkened. Check after 15 minutes—cover the top loosely with aluminum foil if the top seems to be browning too quickly.

Let cool in the pan for 30 minutes before serving with scoops of vanilla ice cream.

For chocolate pecan pie, reduce the amount of honey and sugar to ⅔ cup each, heat with the butter and cinnamon until the butter has melted, then remove from the heat and add 4 oz semisweet dark chocolate, broken into pieces. Let stand for 5 minutes, until the chocolate has melted, then continue as above.

brandied prune & custard tart

Serves **8**

Preparation time **30 minutes**,
  plus standing and chilling

Cooking time **45–50 minutes**

¼ cup **brandy**

2 cups **pitted prunes**
  (dried plums)

⅔ cup **heavy cream**

⅔ cup **milk**

1 **vanilla bean**, slit in half
  lengthwise

1 quantity **pâte sucrée dough**
  (see page 11), chilled

4 **eggs**

¼ cup **superfine sugar**

sifted **confectioners' sugar**,
  for dusting

Warm the brandy in a saucepan, add the prunes, simmer gently for 3–4 minutes, then remove from the heat. Pour the cream and milk into a second saucepan, add the vanilla bean, bring just to a boil, then remove from the heat. Cover both pans and set aside for 2 hours.

Meanwhile, roll the pastry out on a lightly floured surface to fit a buttered 9½ inch loose-bottom fluted tart pan, then press the dough over the bottom and sides. Trim off the excess dough with scissors so that it stands a little above the top of the pan. Prick the bottom with a fork and chill for 15 minutes.

Bake the tart shell blind (see page 15) for 10 minutes. Remove the paper and weights and bake for another 5 minutes. Remove from the oven and reduce the oven temperature to at 350°F.

Beat together the eggs and sugar in a bowl until creamy. Retrieve the vanilla bean, scrape out the seeds, and add the seeds to the eggs, then beat in the milk mixture.

Drain the prunes, adding excess brandy to the milk mixture, then arrange in the bottom of the tart shell. Pour over the custard and bake for 25–30 minutes, until the custard is pale golden and just set. Let cool, then remove from the pan and dust with confectioners' sugar to serve.

For apricot & orange custard tart, make the tart shell as above. Simmer 1½ cups halved dried apricots in the juice of 1 orange and ¼ cup water for 5 minutes. Set aside for 2 hours. Add the grated rind of ½ orange to the custard and make as above. Place the apricots in the shell, pour over the custard, and bake as above.

caramel & chocolate tart

Serves **8**

Preparation time **30 minutes**,
  plus chilling and cooling

Cooking time **20 minutes**

1 quantity **pâte sucrée dough**
  (see page 11), chilled

7 tablespoons **butter**

½ cup firmly packed **dark
  brown sugar**

1⅓ cups **condensed milk**

3 oz **semisweet dark
  chocolate**, broken into
  pieces

3 oz **white chocolate**, broken
  into pieces

Roll the dough out thinly on a lightly floured surface until a little larger than a buttered 8½ inch loose-bottom fluted tart pan. Line the pan (see page 14). Trim off the excess dough with scissors so that it stands a little above the top of the pan. Prick the bottom with a fork, then chill for 15 minutes.

Bake the tart blind (see page 15) for 10 minutes. Remove the paper and weights and cook for another 5–10 minutes or until crisp. Let cool completely.

Heat the butter and sugar in a saucepan until the butter has melted and the sugar dissolved. Add the condensed milk and cook over low heat, stirring for 4–5 minutes, until just beginning to darken and smell of caramel. Pour into the tart shell, spread evenly, and let cool.

Melt the dark and white chocolates in separate bowls set over two small saucepans of just simmering water, making sure that the water does not touch the bottom of the bowls.

Remove the tart from the pan and transfer to a serving plate. Drizzle random spoonfuls of semisweet dark chocolate over the pie. Cool for 10 minutes, then drizzle random spoonfuls of melted white chocolate over the dark layer. Let set. Cut into thin wedges to serve.

For caramel & banana cream tart, fill the tart with caramel filling as above, then cool. Whip 1¼ cups heavy cream and fold in 2 small sliced bananas that have been tossed in the juice of ½ lemon. Spoon over the top of the tart and sprinkle with a little grated semisweet dark chocolate.

208

ginger tarts & coconut rum cream

Makes **12**

Preparation time **30 minutes**,
  plus chilling and cooling

Cooking time **19–23 minutes**

1 quantity **pâte sucrée dough**
  (see page 11), chilled
2 tablespoons **butter**
½ cup firmly packed **light
  brown sugar**
½ cup **light corn syrup**
3 **eggs**, beaten
1 teaspoon **ground ginger**
4 teaspoons chopped
  cyrstallized or **preserved
  ginger**
1 **banana**
grated rind and juice of 1 **lime**

For the coconut rum cream
1¼ cups **heavy cream**
2 tablespoons **confectioners'
  sugar**
¼ cup **white** or **dark rum**
¼ cup **dried flaked coconut**,
  plus extra for sprinkling

Roll the dough out thinly on a lightly floured surface, then stamp out twelve 4 inch circles with a fluted cookie cutter and press into a buttered 12-cup muffin pan, rerolling the dough trimmings as needed. Prick the bottoms of each tart 2–3 times with a fork, then chill for 15 minutes.

Bake the tarts blind (see page 15) for 5 minutes. Remove the paper and weights and cook for another 2–3 minutes. Remove from the oven and reduce the oven temperature to at 350°F.

Add the butter, sugar, and syrup to a medium saucepan and heat gently until the butter has just melted, then let cool slightly. Beat in the eggs, then the ground and chopped ginger. Spoon into the tart shells and bake for 12–15 minutes. Let cool in the pans—the filling will sink and firm up as it cools.

Loosen the tarts with a knife, lift out of the pan, and put on a wire rack, if still warm, or a plate if cold. Make the coconut rum cream by whipping together the cream and confectioners' sugar until it forms soft swirls, then fold in the rum and coconut. Spoon over the top of the tarts.

Peel and slice the banana, then toss with the lime juice. Arrange slices at angles in the cream and sprinkle with lime rind a little extra coconut.

For chocolate tarts & coconut rum cream, omit the ground ginger and chopped ginger from the filling, adding 3 oz semisweet dark chocolate when melting the butter. Add the grated rind of 1 orange to the whipped cream and rum mixture and omit the banana.

white choc & cranberry tart

Makes **6**
Preparation time **30 minutes**,
    plus cooling and chilling
Cooking time **20 minutes**

2 1/2 cups **cranberries**
1/4 cup **superfine sugar**
1/4 cup **crème de cassis**
    or **raspberry liqueur**
7 oz **white chocolate**, broken
    into pieces
1 1/4 cups **ricotta cheese**
1 teaspoon **vanilla extract**
2 tablespoons **cranberry jelly**
6 **store-bought all-butter
    pastry shells**

Gently heat the cranberries, sugar, and crème de cassis in a saucepan for a few minutes until the cranberries are just softened. Strain the cranberries and set aside to cool, reserving the juice.

Melt the white chocolate in a bowl set over a saucepan of barely simmering water, making sure the water does not touch the bottom of the bowl. Stir in the ricotta cheese and vanilla extract and beat together well. Cover and chill.

Add the cranberry jelly to the reserved cranberry juice in the saucepan. Heat gently to melt the jelly and then stir to combine.

Spoon the vanilla and white chocolate mixture into the pastry shells 1–2 hours before serving. Top with the cranberries and spoon the cranberry syrup over to glaze. Chill until needed.

For homemade pastry shells, combine 1 1/3 cups plus 1 tablespoon all-purpose flour with 6 tablespoons butter until the mixture forms crumbs. Add 1/3 cup plus 1 tablespoon confectioners' sugar and 2 egg yolks and mix until a dough forms. Wrap in plastic wrap and chill for 30 minutes. Grease and line the bottom of six 2 1/2 x 3 1/4 inch tart pans with parchment paper. Divide the dough into 6, and press into the pans. Chill for 20 minutes. Trim off the excess dough, line with parchment paper, fill with pie weights or dried beans, then bake in a preheated oven, at 375°F, for 8 minutes. Remove the paper and weights and cook for another 4 minutes, until golden and crisp. Cool in the pans for 10 minutes, then cool on a wire rack before using.

gluten-free

quiches lorraine

Makes **6**

Preparation time **30 minutes**, plus chilling

Cooking time **30–35 minutes**

1 quantity **gluten-free pastry dough** (see page 13)

1 tablespoon **sunflower oil**

4 **smoked bacon slices**, diced

1 small **onion**, chopped

1 cup shredded **sharp cheddar cheese**

3 **eggs**

1 cup **milk**

1 teaspoon **mustard powder**

1 tablespoon chopped **chives** (optional)

salt and **pepper**

Cut the dough into 6, then roll one portion out between 2 sheets of plastic wrap until a little larger than a buttered individual 4 inch loose-bottom fluted tart pan. Remove the top sheet of plastic wrap, turn the dough over, drape into the tart pan, and remove the top sheet of plastic wrap. Press the dough into the bottom and sides of the pan, using your fingers dusted in rice flour. Trim off the excess dough with scissors a little above the top of the pan. Patch any cracks or breaks with dough trimmings. Repeat until 6 tarts have been made. Put on a baking sheet and chill for 15 minutes.

Meanwhile, to make the filling, heat the oil in a skillet, add the bacon and onion, and sauté for 5 minutes, stirring until golden.

Divide three-quarters of the cheese among the tart shells, then sprinkle the onion and bacon mixture on top. Beat the eggs, milk, and mustard in a bowl with a little salt and pepper, then pour into the tarts. Sprinkle with the chives, if using, and the remaining cheese.

Bake the tarts in a preheated oven, at 375°F, for 25–30 minutes, until the tops are golden and the pastry is cooked through. Let cool for 5 minutes, then remove from the pan and serve with salad.

For mushroom quiches, omit the bacon, adding 1½ cups sliced white button mushrooms and 2 tablespoons butter to the lightly fried onions, and sauté for 3–4 minutes, until the mushrooms are just beginning to color. Add the cheese to the tart shells and continue as above.

cheesy picnic pies

Makes **4**
Preparation time **25 minutes**
Cooking time **35 minutes**

1 tablespoon **olive oil**
1 **onion**, chopped
2 **garlic cloves**, finely
   chopped
1 **zucchini**, diced
½ **yellow bell pepper**, seeded
   and diced
½ **red bell pepper**, seeded
   and diced
1⅔ cups canned **diced**
   tomatoes
1 tablespoon chopped
   rosemary or **basil**
½ teaspoon **superfine sugar**
beaten egg, to glaze
salt and **pepper**

For the pastry dough
1 cup **gluten-free bread mix**
6 tablespoons **butter**, diced
1 cup diced **sharp cheddar**
   cheese, plus extra, grated,
   for sprinkling
2 **egg yolks**
2 teaspoons **water**

Heat the oil in a saucepan, add the onion, and sauté for 5 minutes, until softened. Add the garlic, zucchini, and diced bell peppers and sauté briefly, then add the tomatoes, herbs, sugar, and a little salt and pepper. Simmer, uncovered, stirring occasionally, for 10 minutes, until thickened. Cool.

Make the dough. Add the flour, butter, and a little salt and pepper to a bowl, rub in the butter until you have fine crumbs, then stir in the cheese. Add the egg yolks and water and mix to form a smooth dough.

Knead lightly, then cut the dough into 4 pieces. Roll one of the pieces out between 2 sheets of plastic wrap, patting into a neat shape until you have a 7 inch circle. Remove the top sheet of plastic wrap, spoon one-quarter of the filling in the center, brush the dough edges with beaten egg, then fold the dough circle in half while still on the lower piece of plastic wrap.

Peel the dough off the plastic wrap, lift onto an oiled baking sheet, press the edges together well, and press together any breaks in the dough. Repeat with the remaining dough pieces and filling until 4 pies have been made.

Brush with beaten egg, sprinkle with a little extra cheese, and bake in a preheated oven, at 375°F, for 20 minutes, until golden brown. Loosen and transfer to a wire rack. Serve warm or cold with salad.

For ham & tomato picnic pies, omit the red and yellow bell peppers and stir 2 oz cooked ham, diced into the tomato mixture when cold. Continue as above.

cidered chicken pie

Serves **4**

Preparation time **30 minutes**, plus cooling

Cooking time **1½–1¾ hours**

2 tablespoons **butter**

8 **chicken thighs on the bone**

2 **leeks**, trimmed and thickly sliced, white and green parts separated

1¼ cups **chicken stock**

1¼ cups **hard dry cider**

3 sprigs **thyme**, leaves torn from stems

1 tablespoon **cornstarch**, mixed with a little water

4 oz **closed-cup mushrooms**, sliced

1 quantity **gluten-free pastry dough** (see page 13)

beaten egg, to glaze

salt and **pepper**

Heat the butter in a skillet, add the chicken, and sauté on both sides until golden. Remove from the skillet and set aside. Add the white leek slices to the skillet and sauté for 2–3 minutes, until softened. Return the chicken to the skillet, add the stock, cider, and thyme, then season with salt and pepper. Bring to a boil, cover, and simmer for 45 minutes, until the chicken is cooked through.

Transfer the chicken to a plate. Stir the cornstarch mixture into the skillet and bring to a boil, stirring until thickened, then remove from the heat. Remove the skin and bones from the chicken, dice the meat, and add to the sauce with the green leeks and mushrooms. Let cool.

Spoon the filling into the bottom of a 1¼ quart pie plate. Roll out the dough between 2 sheets of plastic wrap for the lid. Brush the rim of the plate with beaten egg.

Remove one sheet of plastic wrap, lay the dough over the plate, then remove the top sheet of wrap. Press the dough onto the plate using fingers dusted with rice flour. Trim off the excess, then brush with beaten egg. Bake in a preheated oven, at 375°F, for 30–35 minutes, until the pastry is golden and the filling is piping hot.

For chicken & tarragon pie, sauté the chicken as above, then drain and sauté the white leek slices with 4 diced smoked bacon slices until golden. Add ⅔ cup dry white wine, 2 cups chicken stock, salt, and pepper, omitting the thyme. Cover and simmer, thicken as above, then add the green leek slices, 1 tablespoon chopped tarragon, and 2 tablespoons chopped parsley, omitting the mushrooms. Spoon into the plate and continue as above.

sausage & caramelized onion rolls

Makes **8**
Preparation time **30 minutes**
Cooking time **35–40 minutes**

1 tablespoon **olive oil**
1 **onion**, thinly sliced
1 **garlic clove**, finely chopped
1 teaspoon **superfine sugar**
1 **apple**, quartered, cored, peeled
8 oz **ground pork**
1 **egg yolk**
8 **sage leaves**
1 quantity **gluten-free pastry dough** (see page 13)
beaten egg, to glaze
salt and **pepper**

Heat the oil in a skillet, add the onion, and sauté gently for 10 minutes, until softened. Add the garlic and sugar, increase the heat slightly, and sauté, stirring more frequently, for another 5 minutes, until a deep golden.

Add the apple to a food processor and finely chop. Add the pork, egg yolk, sage, and plenty of salt and pepper and process. (Alternatively, finely chop the apple and sage, then mix with pork, egg yolk, and seasoning.)

Roll out half the dough between 2 sheets of plastic wrap to a 12 × 4 inch strip. Remove the top plastic wrap and spoon half the onion mixture in a line down the center, then spoon half the ground pork in a line on top. Brush the edges of the dough with beaten egg.

Fold the dough strip in half to enclose the filling and press the edges together, using fingers dusted with rice flour to seal well. Trim the edges to tidy up, then cut the strips into pieces about 3 inches thick. Arrange slightly spaced apart on an oiled baking sheet. Repeat with the remaining dough, onion, and pork mixture.

Make 2–3 small slashes in the top of each sausage roll, brush with beaten egg to glaze, then bake in a preheated oven, at 375°F, for 20–25 minutes, until the pastry is golden and the filling cooked through. Transfer to a wire rack and let cool.

For plain sausage rolls, roll out half the dough as above, arrange 3 skinned, gluten-free herb sausages on top, brush the edge with egg, then fold over, seal, and cut into pieces. Repeat with the remaining dough and an additional 3 sausages. Cut into pieces and bake as above.

beef & mustard pies

Makes **4**
Preparation time **30 minutes**,
  plus cooling
Cooking time **about 2½ hours**

1 tablespoon **sunflower oil**
1½ lb **chuck short ribs** or
  boneless beef chuck, any
  fat discarded and diced
4 **smoked bacon slices**,
  diced
1 **onion**, chopped
1 cup **red wine**
1¾ cups **beef stock**
1 tablespoon **tomato paste**
2 teaspoons **mustard powder**
6 **bay leaves**
1 tablespoon **cornstarch**,
  mixed with a little water
2 tablespoons **butter**
8 oz **shallots**, halved if large
1 quantity **gluten-free pastry
  dough** (see page 13) with
  1 teaspoon mustard powder
  added
beaten egg, to glaze
salt and **pepper**

Heat the oil in a skillet and add the beef, a few pieces at a time, until it has all been added to the skillet. Cook over high heat, stirring until browned on all sides. Lift out of the skillet and transfer to a casserole dish.

Sauté the bacon and onion until golden, then add the wine, stock, tomato paste, and mustard powder. Add 2 bay leaves and season generously with salt and pepper. Add the cornstarch mixture, bring to a boil, stirring until thickened, then pour over the beef.

Cover the casserole dish and bake in a preheated oven, at 350°F, for 2 hours, until the beef is tender. Heat the butter in a clean skillet and sauté the shallots for about 5 minutes, until golden. Add to the beef casserole and let cool. Discard the bay leaves.

Divide the beef mixture among 4 individual 1¼ cup pie plates. Cut the dough into 4, and roll one piece out between 2 sheets of plastic wrap to make a pie lid. Brush the rim of a plate with beaten egg, remove one sheet of plastic wrap, lay the dough over the plate, then remove the top sheet of plastic wrap. Press the dough onto the plate edge, using fingers dusted with rice flour. Trim off the excess dough and fork the edge. Repeat until 4 pies have been made. Brush with egg, add a bay leaf to each for decoration (do not eat), then bake in a preheated oven, at 375°F, for 20–25 minutes, until the pastry is golden and the filling piping hot.

For beery beef & mustard pies, omit the red wine and add 1¼ cups bitter or other strong beer and 1¼ cups beef stock. Omit the shallots and add 3 sliced portabello mushrooms. Continue as above.

glazed apple tart

Serves **8**

Preparation time **30 minutes**, plus chilling

Cooking time **1 hour–1 hour 10 minutes**

1 quantity **sweet gluten-free pastry dough** (see page 13)

3 **cooking apples** (about 1¼ lb)

⅔ cup **superfine sugar**

3 **eggs**

grated rind and juice of 1 **lemon**

2 tablespoons **marmalade**

Press the just-made dough over the bottom and sides of a buttered 9½ inch loose-bottom fluted tart pan, using fingers dusted in rice flour, until the dough is an even thickness and stands a little above the top of the pan. Trim with scissors to tidy up, if needed. Prick the bottom with a fork, put on a baking sheet, and chill for 15 minutes.

Line the tart shell with nonstick parchment paper, add pie weights or dried beans, and bake blind in a preheated oven, at 375°F, for 10 minutes. Remove the paper and weights and cook for another 5 minutes. Reduce the oven temperature to 350°F.

Quarter, core, and peel the apples, cut into thin slices, and arrange slightly overlapping in rings over the bottom of the tart, then top with a second layer. Reserve 2 tablespoons of the sugar for the topping, then mix the rest with the eggs and lemon rin, and juice, beating with a fork until smooth. Pour over the apples.

Sprinkle with the remaining sugar, then bake for 40–45 minutes, until the apples are browned and the pastry shell is cooked through. Brush the marmalade over the top, return the tart to the oven, and bake for another 5–10 minutes, until glistening.

For glazed apricot tart, fill the baked blind tart shell (as above, see page 15) with 12 halved and pitted apricots (about 1 lb). Mix 3 eggs with ⅓ cup sugar and the grated rind and juice of 1 lemon, then pour over the apricots. Sprinkle with 2 tablespoons sugar and bake as above. Glaze with 2 tablespoons warmed apricot preserves after cooking.

lemon meringue pies

Makes **6**

Preparation time **30 minutes**, plus chilling

Cooking time **25–30 minutes**

1 quantity **sweet gluten-free pastry dough** (see page 13)

1 1/3 cups canned **condensed milk**

3 **egg yolks**

grated rind of 2 **lemons**

1/4 cup **lemon juice**

4 **egg whites**

2/3 cup **superfine sugar**

Cut the dough into 6, then roll one portion out between 2 sheets of plastic wrap until a little larger than a buttered 4 inch loose-bottom fluted tart pan. Remove one sheet of plastic wrap, lay the dough over the pan, then remove the top sheet of plastic wrap. Press the dough into the bottom and sides of the pan, using fingers dusted with rice flour. Trim off the excess dough with scissors so that it stands a little above the top of the pan. Patch any cracks or breaks with dough trimmings. Repeat to make 6 tarts. Prick the bottoms with a fork, then chill for 15 minutes.

Bake the tarts blind (see page 15) for 10 minutes. Remove the paper and weights and cook for another 5 minutes. Remove from the oven and reduce the oven temperature to at 350°F.

Mix together the condensed milk, egg yolks, and lemon rind and juice in a bowl until the mixture thickens, then spoon the filling into the tart shells. In a second bowl, whisk the egg whites until stiff, then gradually whisk in the sugar, a little at a time, until thick and glossy.

Spoon the meringue over the filling and swirl with the back of a spoon into peaks. Bake for 10–15 minutes, until the peaks are golden and just set. Let stand for 5 minutes, remove from the pans, and serve warm or cold with cream.

For St. Clements meringue pies, mix the condensed milk with the egg yolks, grated rinds of 1 orange, 1 lime, and 1 lemon, and 1/4 cup of mixed fruit juice. Spoon into the 6 baked tart shells. Make the meringue with 4 egg whites and 1/3 cup superfine sugar mixed with 1/3 cup firmly packed light brown sugar. Bake as above.

banana & caramel pie

Serves **6**
Preparation time **25 minutes**,
   plus chilling
Cooking time **4–5 minutes**

5 tablespoons **butter**
1 tablespoon **light corn syrup**
1¼ cups crushed **gluten-free
   cookies** (place the cookies
   in a plastic bag and use a
   rolling pin to crush)
1¼ cups **heavy cream**
2 **bananas**
juice of ½ **lemon**

For the caramel filling
¼ lb (1 stick) **butter**
½ cup firmly packed **dark
   brown sugar**
1 (14 oz) can **condensed
   milk**

To decorate
diced **caramels**
grated **chocolate** (optional)

Melt the butter in a saucepan with the syrup, remove
from the heat, and stir in the cookie crumbs. Transfer
to an unbuttered 8 inch loose-bottom fluted tart pan,
then press over the bottom and up the sides with the
back of a spoon to make into an even layer. Chill for
30 minutes.

Make the caramel filling. Melt the butter in a clean,
dry saucepan with the sugar, add the condensed milk,
and stir well, then bring to a boil and cook over medium
heat for 4–5 minutes, stirring continously, until the
mixture begins to thicken, smells of caramel, and
crystallizes around the edges. Be careful not to
overheat because the milk can scorch easily.

Pour the caramel into the pie shell, let cool, then chill
for 3½-4½ hours or until ready to serve.

Whip the cream until it forms soft swirls. Slice the
bananas and toss with the lemon juice, then fold into
the cream and spoon over the pie. Decorate the top
with diced caramels and grated chocolate, if desired.
Serve within 2 hours of decorating.

For caramel chocolate pie, make the pie shell
and caramel layer as above. Melt 4 oz semisweet dark
chocolate in a bowl over hot water, then stir in the
(unwhipped) cream and 2 tablespoons confectioners'
sugar. Chill for 30 minutes, then beat until just
beginning to thicken, spoon over the caramel layer,
and sprinkle with coarsely chopped, toasted hazelnuts.

pear & frangipane tart

Serves **6-8**
Preparation time **30 minutes**,
  plus chilling
Cooking time **45–55 minutes**

1 quantity **sweet gluten-free
  pastry dough** (see page 13)
¼ lb (1 stick) **butter**, at room
  temperature
⅔ cup **superfine sugar**
1¼ cups **ground almonds**
2 **eggs**
few drops of **almond extract**
4 oz **semisweet dark
  chocolate**, diced
4 ripe **pears**, quartered, cored,
  peeled, and thickly sliced
juice of ½ **lemon**
2 tablespoons **slivered
  almonds**
sifted **confectioners' sugar**,
  for dusting

Press the just-made dough over the bottom and up
the sides of a buttered 9½ inch loose-bottom fluted
tart pan, using fingers dusted in rice flour, until the
dough stands a little above the top of the pan. Trim
with scissors to tidy up. Prick the bottom with a fork,
put on a baking sheet, and chill for 15 minutes.

Bake the tart blind (see page 15) for 10 minutes.
Remove the paper and weights and cook for another
5 minutes. Remove from the oven and reduce the
oven temperature to at 350°F.

Cream the butter and sugar together until light and
fluffy. Add the ground almonds, eggs, and almond
extract and beat until smooth. Fold in half the chocolate.

Toss the pears in the lemon juice and arrange half in
a random pattern in the bottom of the tart. Spoon the
almond frangipane over the top and spread as evenly
as you can. Press the remaining pears into the filling,
then sprinkle with the slivered almonds. Bake for
30–40 minutes, until the frangipane is golden and just
set. Check after 20 minutes and cover the top loosely
with aluminum foil if the almonds seem to be browning
too quickly. Let cool for 30 minutes.

Remove the tart from the pan, sprinkle with the
remaining chocolate, and dust with confectioners' sugar.
Serve warm or cold.

For chocolate sauce to serve as an accompaniment,
break 4 oz dark chocolate into pieces and melt in a bowl
set over a saucepan of gently simmering water with
4 tablespoons unsalted butter and 1 tablespoon light
corn syrup. Cool slightly, then spoon over the tart.

mincemeat, apricot & apple pies

Makes **12**
Preparation time **30 minutes**
Cooking time **20 minutes**

1 quantity **sweet gluten-free pastry dough** (see page 13) flavored with 1 teaspoon ground cinnamon
½ cup **gluten-free fruit mincemeat**
½ cup diced **dried apricots**
1 **apple**, peeled, cored, and finely chopped
egg white, to glaze
sifted **confectioners' sugar**, for dusting

Reserve one-third of the dough. Cut the rest in half, and roll one half out between 2 sheets of plastic wrap until ¼ inch thick. Stamp out as many circles as you can with a 2½ inch fluted cookie cutter, peel off the plastic wrap, and press into the buttered sections of a 12-cup muffin pan, using fingers dusted with rice flour. Roll out the other dough half and repeat until you have 12 pie shells. Add the trimmings to the reserved dough.

Mix the mincemeat with the apricots and apple, then spoon into the pie shells. Roll out the remaining dough between plastic wrap as before, then cut out twelve 2 inch star shapes, add to the top of the pies, and brush with egg white.

Bake the pies in a preheated oven, at 375°F, for about 20 minutes, until golden. Let stand for 10 minutes, then loosen the edges with a small knife and lift out of the pan (the pies are more crumbly than those made with wheat flour, so be careful). Let cool completely on a wire rack, then dust with confectioners' sugar before serving.

For almond mince pies, add ¼ cup ground almonds to the dough instead of the ground cinnamon. Top the filling with ⅓ cup slivered almonds, then bake as above, covering with aluminum foil after 15 minutes if the almonds seem to be browning too quickly. Dust with confectioners' sugar to serve.

index

acknowledgments

Executive editor Eleanor Maxfield
Senior editor Sybella Stephens
Art direction & design Tracy Killick
Photographer Stephen Conroy
Home economist Sara Lewis
Prop stylist Rachel Jukes
Production Caroline Alberti

Photography copyright © Octopus Publishing Group
Limited/Stephen Conroy, except the following:
copyright © Octopus Publishing Group/David Munns
105; Ian Wallace 167, 189, 195, 199, 201;
Lis Parsons 57, 83, 169; Will Heap 15-17, 53, 133,
137, 141, 149, 153, 179, 193, 203, 214;
William Shaw 39, 47, 58, 91, 107, 120, 160, 187.